ERASMUS
LECTURES AND WAYFARING
SKETCHES

P. S. Allen

From the portrait by Herbert Olivier 1929
in the President's Lodgings, Corpus Christi College, Oxford

ERASMUS
LECTURES AND WAYFARING SKETCHES

BY

P. S. ALLEN

LATE PRESIDENT OF
CORPUS CHRISTI COLLEGE, OXFORD

OXFORD
AT THE CLARENDON PRESS
1934

OXFORD
UNIVERSITY PRESS
AMEN HOUSE, E.C. 4
London Edinburgh Glasgow
New York Toronto Melbourne
Capetown Bombay Calcutta
Madras Shanghai
HUMPHREY MILFORD
PUBLISHER TO THE
UNIVERSITY

PRINTED IN GREAT BRITAIN

PREFACE

IT was my husband's intention to publish a second
volume of collected lectures and papers similar to the
Age of Erasmus. In the quiet of a summer's visit to
Ottery St. Mary he began to make selection: but the
double work for Corpus and for Erasmus left him no
time to finish. He had often been asked to write
Erasmus' life and would answer that that must wait
till the letters were edited. Once, at the entreaty of a
friend, who begged that those who cannot read the Latin
might also be considered, he started to write; but he
had no leisure to continue. There are, however, several
lectures on Erasmus and on his work which give a picture of him, of the people he lived among and the places
he passed through. These my husband grouped together
at the beginning of the volume, to be followed by papers
on subjects connected with the period. At the end he
put the sketches made on our travels, 'Erasmian Way-
farings' as Mr. Garrod has called them.

'Erasmus', the first lecture printed here, was delivered
at Liverpool for the Department of Education; and
repeated immediately afterwards in Holland, at Rotterdam, Utrecht, Leiden, Amsterdam, and Haarlem, where
my husband was invited to lecture in the spring of 1922.
After the lecture at Amsterdam a telegram was handed
to him, announcing that the University of Leiden wished
to confer on him an honorary doctorate, a rare honour;
his predecessors from Oxford were Lord Bryce and
Jowett. It was characteristic that on his return he only
mentioned the degree to his family: 'I fear I shall be
puffed up', he said.

'Erasmus' Services to Learning', a lecture to the British

Academy, and 'The Writings of Erasmus' describe Erasmus' work for scholarship. 'The Writings of Erasmus' Mr. Garrod has skilfully put together from two incomplete lectures. The first of these was given to the English school in Oxford on 8 February 1913, and repeated to the Socratic Club and English Society in Birmingham the same month. The end of the lecture has disappeared, but its substance was incorporated in an address many years later to the Oxford Clerical Society. 'Erasmus on Church Unity' is a paper read to the same society in March 1925. It explains Erasmus' position towards the Reformation and his conviction that the ills of the Church were to be remedied by agreement in goodness. In order that Erasmus might speak for himself my husband translated the last part of the *Liber De Sarcienda Ecclesiae Concordia*, published in 1533 but never before translated into English. 'Erasmus' Relations with his Printers' is a paper read to the Bibliographical Society in London in March 1915. 'Erasmus' Servant-Pupils' was not given as a lecture; it seems it may have been a fragment of the 'Life'. It shows Erasmus in his home, when the boy who was afterwards the famous Bishop Gardiner prepared his lettuces with vinegar and butter.

The second group of lectures are: 'Trilingual Colleges of the Early Sixteenth Century', read to the Classical Association in London on 11 December 1916; and 'Christopher Plantin and his Circle', an address given at Antwerp on 9 August 1920 for the celebration of the four-hundredth anniversary of Plantin's birth.

The last group are the sketches made on our travels. We went to Alcalá because of Ximenes' university; to Coca because the Fonsecas were buried there; to Simancas to search for Erasmus' letters—and we found an unknown one to him from Charles V, rejoicing that he was resisting Lutheranism and exhorting him to take care of his health. Provins we visited because Dr. William Hunt told us of its beauty; Montbenoît because Ferry Carondelet held the Abbey; Thann because there a packet of Erasmus' letters went astray. Hungary we had visited before for friendship's sake, but our last visit was to seek the letter-book of Erasmus' correspondent, Nicholas Oláh, Archbishop of Esztergom and Chancellor to Ferdinand. We found it after many vicissitudes and were treated with princely generosity by the owner. We made systematic, sometimes repeated, visits to the libraries of the English cathedrals; among these Durham holds a distinguished place.

Had my husband edited these papers he might have cut out repetitions and enriched the lectures with further detail. It seemed our part to give them to the reader so far as possible as they are.

HELEN MARY ALLEN

22 MANOR PLACE, OXFORD.

7 *July* 1934.

BIBLIOGRAPHICAL NOTE

'Erasmus' printed by the Department of Education, Liverpool.

'Erasmus' Services to Learning', from the *Proceedings of the British Academy*, vol. xi.

'Erasmus' Relations with his Printers', from the *Transactions of the Bibliographical Society*, vol. xiii.

Alcalá, the *Pelican Record*, June 1912.

A Castle in Spain, the *Oxford Magazine*, 19 February 1914.

Provins, *The Times*, 24 August 1920.

CONTENTS

DATES OF ERASMUS' LIFE: 27 Oct. 1466–12 July 1536.

1466–75. Born at Rotterdam: at school at Gouda: Chorister at Utrecht.

1475–84. At school at Deventer.
At school at Hertogenbosch.

1487?–94. An Augustinian at Steyn, near Gouda: Antibarbari. Secretary to the Bishop of Cambray.

1495–9. Paris: De ratione studii, De copia, De conscribendis epistolis, Colloquiorum formulae, Paraphrase of Valla's Elegantiae.

May 1499–Jan. 1500. England. Oct.–Dec. 1499. Oxford: Disputatiuncula.

1500–5. Paris: Collectanea Adagiorum, Cicero, Jerome, Enchiridion.
(1502–4. Louvain: Translations of Libanius, Euripides; Panegyricus, Valla's Annotations on N.T.)

1505–June 1506. England. London: Translations of N.T., Lucian, Euripides. April 1506. Cambridge.

1506–9. Italy. Bologna, Venice, Rome: Adagiorum Chiliades, De pueris instituendis.

1509–July 1514. England. London: Moriae Encomium.
(April–June 1511. Paris.)
Aug. 1511–Jan. 1514. Cambridge: New Testament, Jerome, Seneca, Plutarch, De copia, Cato.
[1512. Living of Aldington given by Warham; commuted to a pension.]

Aug. 1514–May 1516. Basle: Institutio principis, Ratio verae theologiae, Paraclesis, Gaza.
(April–May 1515, July–Aug. 1516. London.)
[1516. Councillor to Prince Charles; in receipt of pension. Prebend at Courtray given by Le Sauvage: commuted to a pension.]

Sept. 1516–June 1517. Antwerp, Brussels, Ghent: Querela Pacis.
(April 1517. London.)

July 1517–Oct. 1521. Louvain: Suetonius, Curtius, Paraphrases, New Testament, Cyprian.
(May–Sept. 1518, Basle. Oct.–Nov. 1520, Aachen, Cologne. May–Oct. 1521, Anderlecht. Aug. 1521, Bruges.)

Nov. 1521–April 1529.   Basle: Paraphrases, Colloquia, Hilary, Precatio Dominica, Exomologesis, Lingua,
 Institutio Christiani matrimonii, Irenaeus, Ambrose, De pronuntiatione, Ciceronianus, Augustine, Chrysostom.
April 1529–June 1535.   Freiburg: Consultatio, De ciuilitate, Aristotle, Basil, De Ecclesiae concordia, De
 praeparatione ad mortem, Ecclesiastes.
 [1533. Pension given by the Duke of
 Cleves.]
 1535–6.   Basle: De puritate, Origen.

NOTE.—Erasmus' writings are assigned here to the periods in which they were
 originally or mainly composed.

PRINCIPAL WORKS, AS PUBLISHED

LITERARY.

Adagia, 1500, 1506, 1508, 1515,
 1518, 1520, 1523, 1526, 1528,
 1533, 1536.
Moriae Encomium, 1511.
Julius Exclusus, 1513.
Parabolae, 1514.
Epistolae, 1515, 1516, 1517, 1518,
 1519, 1521, 1528, 1529, 1531,
 1532, 1534, 1536.
Antibarbari, 1520.
Colloquia, 1522–33.
Dialogus de recta Latini Grae-
 cique sermonis pronuntia-
 tione, 1528.
Ciceronianus, 1528.
Apophthegmata, 1531.

Cicero, Off., 1501, 1520.
Seneca, 1515, 1529.
Suetonius, 1518, 1533.
Curtius, 1518.
Aristotle, 1531.
Ptolemy, 1533.

Libanius, 1503 ⎫
Euripides, 1506 ⎪
Lucian, 1506 ⎬ translated.
Plutarch, 1514 ⎪
Galen, 1526   ⎪
Xenophon, 1530 ⎭

EDUCATIONAL.

De ratione studii, 1511.
De copia, 1512.
De constructione, 1515.
Colloquiorum formulae, 1519.
De conscribendis epistolis, 1522.
De pueris instituendis, 1529.
De ciuilitate, 1530.
Paraphrase of Valla's Elegantiae,
 1531.

Cato, &c., 1514.
Gaza's Greek grammar, 1516.

DIVINITY.

Disputatiuncula, 1503.
Commentaries on Psalms, 1515–32.
Paraphrases of N.T., 1517–24.

Valla's Annotations on N.T., 1505
New Testament, 1516, 1519, 1522,
 1527, 1535.
Jerome, 1516, 1524, 1533.
Cyprian, 1520.
Arnobius, 1522.
Hilary, 1523.
Irenaeus, 1526.
Ambrose, 1527.
Augustine, 1528–9.
Lactantius, 1529.

Chrysostom (Lat.), 1530, 1536.
Alger, 1530.
Basil (Lat.), 1532.
Haymo, 1533.
Origen, 1536.

Vidua Christiana, 1529.
Explanatio symboli, 1533.
De praeparatione ad mortem, 1534.
Ecclesiastes, 1535.

MORAL AND RELIGIOUS.

Enchiridion militis Christiani, 1503, 1518.
Ratio verae theologiae, 1518.
Paraclesis, 1519.
Precatio Dominica, 1523.
Exomologesis, 1524.
Modus orandi Deum, 1524.
Lingua, 1525.
Institutio Christiani matrimonii, 1526.

POLITICAL

Panegyricus, 1504.
Institutio principis Christiani, 1516.
Bellum
Sileni Alcibiadis } (from Adagia)
Scarabeus   1517.
Querela Pacis, 1517.
Consultatio de bello Turcico, 1530
De Ecclesiae concordia, 1533.
De puritate Ecclesiae, 1536.

NOTE.—Most of these Erasmus frequently revised and reissued. In a few of the more notable cases the dates of the new editions are shown.

ERASMUS

It is often asked, What did Erasmus do? Why are people so interested in him? His is one of the great names of the world, known to many who do not occupy themselves with history or with learning, and whose mind is not to read books; and yet it is not easy to say in a few words to what he owes his eminence. His was no definite life's work. He ruled no kingdom, won no battles to decide the fate of nations; built no bridges, nor a city to be called after his name. Avoiding persecution, he won no martyr's crown. No discoveries are associated with him, he led no new movement of thought. His writings are indeed voluminous; but mere bulk is not apt to bring fame, and even if it were, how few of his books are now read! Students still turn over the great folios which made his reputation, though not for the purpose for which they were written; but the literary world knows little more than the trifles which he threw off to amuse himself, and of which he never ventured to be proud.

Before setting out to answer the questions with which I began, let us first glance shortly at the facts of his life. Until he went to Paris in 1495 he had scarcely left the confines of Holland. Education in the famous school of Deventer should have led him to a university; but orphaned and poor, he had to make for himself the way which his talents imperiously demanded. Drifting into a monastery, he extricated himself before it was too late, and at the age of twenty-nine found himself free to study in the great centre of Transalpine learning. In those days men might die of old age at fifty: already, it must have seemed, a precious slice of his life was gone. The fire burned hot within him; but what had he yet achieved?

In this connexion one point may be made. By the time he came to Paris he had read a great deal of the Latin classics, and had already begun to form his incomparable style: this therefore he had done in Holland. The monasteries which he so disliked had given him opportunities; the long convivial meals he hated had not prevented the young canon of Steyn from raiding any library that came in his way, and from carrying off to his cell books to be devoured in the peace of long summer dawns or westering suns.

Once free, wherever he went, he made friends. His was not the gentle goodness which looks away from evil and turns the wicked man from his wickedness. Serious purpose he had, to serve God with all his strength, in spite of the frail body which from the first hampered him and in the end gave him the pains of martyrdom. Wit, brilliance, charm, quick thought and ready tongue, and that open confidence which disarms—all these were his; and he smiled his way into men's hearts long before they realized his wonderful powers. An English pupil bore him off to England in 1499; where, for all his hood and tonsure, he shone in the hunting-field and made conquests among the ladies. At court a few minutes' conversation made the future king of England his friend for life: at Oxford he captivated the austere Colet, even when opposing him and refusing an invitation to stay and work side by side. After a few more years of struggle with poverty Erasmus had learnt Greek; and then began his time of fruitfulness, never to cease in the thirty years of life remaining.

His first work with his hard-won talent was to make a new translation of the New Testament; dwelling in Colet's house in London, and using manuscripts supplied from the library of St. Paul's Cathedral, of which his friend was Dean. Then came the chance which the young

Dutchman had longed for all his life, from the day when his schoolmaster had laid his hand on the boy's head at Deventer and foretold—more truly than he imagined—the glory that was to come. Italy, home of the Muses, was the goal to which every Northern scholar turned his eyes; and to Erasmus the dream till now had never come true. He grasped the position offered him, not a pleasant one, and was quickly disillusioned. Julius II, taking Bologna by storm, created on this critical observer an impression which flattering receptions by Cardinals in Rome failed to remove. For a year he sat at Venice in the house of Messer Aldo, writing his first great book, the *Adagia*; and at the end he realized that he was a match in scholarship for anything that Italy could show.

Disappointed here, he caught again at opportunity. The young prince, on whom he had smiled ten years ago, succeeded to the throne of England; and his pupil-patron, Lord Mountjoy, joined with the Archbishop of Canterbury in bidding him come back and bask in the sunshine that had broken over the land. For five years he divided his time between Cambridge and London, doing the work which was to bring him almost at one step to the pinnacle of fame, the acknowledged leader of learning in Europe. Then in 1514 he sought the acquaintance of Froben, and at Basle again made a circle of friendships which only death could sever. The books he had been preparing for, came out; Seneca, Jerome and the New Testament—the first edition ever published (though not the first printed) in the Greek—, and his reputation was made. Thenceforward Erasmus needed no patrons: he could choose whom he would to honour with his presence, and he chose none. Prince Charles of Spain made him a councillor, and was proud to have him settle at Louvain; but when the need arose again to be at the printers' side,

Erasmus went off to Basle, his own master at the price of his Imperial pension unpaid.

His last years at Basle and Freiburg were greatly productive, though his poor body suffered more and more; the stone keeping him face to face with death for months at a time. From one bout of torture after another he rose up again to his work. His pen flew on as fast, biting as keenly as ever into the subjects before him. Enormous editions of the Fathers issued from the press, the text corrected and annotated by Erasmus, and prefaced with brilliant essays of exposition—Cyprian, Hilary, Jerome again, Irenaeus, Ambrose, Augustine, Chrysostom in Latin, Jerome for the third time; and at the end he had Origen in hand, and left him for his faithful executors to finish. Besides these he re-edited his New Testament four times; and on every book of it but the Revelation wrote eloquent Paraphrases, which have comforted pious readers in many lands. The tale of his lesser works and his own compositions seems almost without an end.

This then is what Erasmus did; but we must not look here for the answer to our second question, Why are people so interested in him? The work that he did abides, but we heed it not. It is the foundation of modern critical study of the Bible and the Fathers, but it receives no more attention than do the foundations of mighty buildings, strong and true but underground and out of sight. It has been said of Erasmus that he propounded the problem of criticism, but did little himself to solve it; and it must be confessed that this latter part is true enough. But his failings were the failings of his time— an age when archaeology and palaeography were in their cradles, and when textual criticism knew only the boldest and most dashing methods. His merit was to perceive that the invention of printing had brought in a new era of critical study, when a text once well and truly fashioned to embody the sum of existing knowledge could become a tool for hundreds of scholars, identical and invariable, on which each could rely, knowing that his friend was using precisely the same; also a standard by which new-found manuscripts could be tested. And thus the quest of critical accuracy moved at one bound to a higher plane. Yet not for this does the world praise and love him to-day.

Besides Erasmus the steadfast scholar, there was another Erasmus of whom we have not spoken. The flashing wit which enlivened his serious purpose could not be hidden under a bushel. On his long rides from Italy to England in 1509, his thoughts turned to a charming friend whom he was soon to see again; and More's name suggested a contrast between so wise a person and the many fools over whom the literary fashion of the day was making merry. The outcome of his thoughts, put together as he lay sick in More's happy home in Bucklersbury, was a Lucianic composition, *Moriae Encomium,* a Praise of Folly, in which with exquisite ingenuity he extolled the absurdities of life and those that practise them, while his duller victims never suspected that praise so subtle was blame. This was followed a year or two later by a stinging satire on the Pope, whom he had seen emulating his namesake, the Caesar whom the world knew as irresistible conqueror. Julius Exclusus, shut out from heaven by his uncompromising predecessor St. Peter, was a pretty spectacle of humiliated rage; his thunderbolts reduced to impotence and himself obliged to submit. Under his own name Erasmus never dared to publish it; but its success was immediate, and he was encouraged to go on. In his later years, 1522–33, he poured out a number of similar Colloquies, which are still

delightful to read. To the student of history no small part
of their interest is the vivid light that they throw on the
life of the times; enhanced now and again by an episode
which is evidently adapted, with the thinnest disguise,
from Erasmus' own experience. But a more permanent
factor in their life is the clever dialogue, the brisk thrust
and parry, the skilful elaboration of character, the good
humour and, according to the standards of his time, if
not of ours, the delicacy.

These works, the *Praise of Folly* and the *Colloquies*,
we read to-day; and men will continue to enjoy them as
long as the art of reading is practised. Yet neither for
them is Erasmus great in Europe. We will pause for a
few minutes to consider the rise of his fame. When did
he first become a personage of importance to the world
at large? He first got his name into print in his early days
in Paris, by offering the printers a letter of compliment
with which to fill the end pages of Gaguin's History of
France. That much-respected leader of the world of
letters in Paris was too ill to supervise his own book as it
went through the press; so that the intervention of a
young aspirant to public notice was the easier. But it
was not resented. Two or three years later Gaguin published a collection of his letters, and included three which
he had written about that time to 'Herasmus, Austin
Canon'; not foreseeing that posterity would be more
interested in his undistinguished correspondent than in
himself. In 1503 Erasmus received the dedication of a
book, some poems of the great schoolmaster at Deventer,
Alexander Hegius, edited by James Faber, pupil of
Hegius in the school and then teacher there. But this
was the act of a personal friend, and is no evidence of
general reputation. In January 1504, when he delivered
his Panegyric to the Archduke Philip at Brussels—an

occasion which no doubt he had made for himself—,to the treasury officials who paid him his reward, 50 livres, he was nothing more than 'Vng religieux de l'ordre de Saint Augustin'. In October when he had again attained his purpose, further alms from the Archduke 'to entertain him at the schools of Louvain', to the same officials he had acquired a name, 'Frère Erasme Rotherdamensis', but the description is the same, 'religieux de l'ordre de Saint Augustin'; there was nothing to distinguish him in their eyes, and in the eyes of other people, from the many religious who were to be seen standing in the ante-rooms of kings.

Through the next years, when he was visiting Paris again and England and Italy, his fame was steadily rising; and the publication of the *Adagiorum Chiliades* by Aldus in 1508 put a seal upon it. The book was clearly *magistral*. The learning which it displayed was immense. The whole field of Greek and Latin literature had been explored; and every kind of proverb or literary allusion was set out, for use by those who aspired to embellish their Latin writing with elegant ornament. To write in Latin at that period was an indispensable accomplishment for anyone who wrote at all; so that the book appealed to a wide public and was in continual demand, re-edited again and again up to the last years of its author's life.

But there is another feature in it which may be noted as illustrative of Erasmus' character. The books he had published hitherto had been simple and straightforward, their nature clearly shown upon their faces: *Collectanea Adagiorum*, the germ of the present work, 800 proverbs with a line or two of interpretation to each; *Enchiridion Militis Christiani*, a handbook of practical piety; the Panegyric on Philip; translations from Lucian and

Euripides. But in the *Chiliades* a new vein appears, a vein which was to run through all the rest of his work. Instead of confining himself to his subject he begins to expatiate as occasion arises, on whatever interests him. He takes the world into his confidence, thinking aloud with complete absence of self-consciousness. 'Quicquid in buccam venerit', whatever came into his mouth, out came the words and flowed straight on to the paper before him : reminiscences of his own life; pleasant commendations of his friends; praise of his dear Holland with the stately ships coming in to the mart of the whole world; notes on foreign customs and peculiarities of pronunciation; tales of what he had seen on his travels; discourses on matters political and ecclesiastical, moral and religious; reproof of kings who plunder their subjects and make war on their neighbours; censure of niggard owners who keep their manuscripts to themselves and will not allow them to be printed; exposure of fraud or imposture among high or low, rich or poor.

With each new edition of the book this element increases; and it spreads into all that he wrote. His notes on the New Testament and on the Fathers are full of such disquisitions: the characters in his Colloquies tell stories of what he had seen and known, the first marriage of Thomas More, games with the Colts at Netherhall, a visit to Henry VIII at Richmond, the magnificent Certosa at Pavia, recollections of Standonck's College at Paris, of sceptical pilgrimages to Walsingham and Canterbury. Whatever his subject, the Right Mode of Prayer, the Right Use of the Tongue, Christian Marriage, the Christian Widow, Counsel about War with the Turk, or about healing the Dissension in the Church; at any moment he may break off into some episode, light and entertaining or instinct with serious warning, which his headlong thought has suggested to him as his pen runs on. Two years after his death a worthy Franciscan published his Notes on the New Testament in a compressed form; stating in a preface that the matter was too valuable to be neglected, but that he considered it more decorous to cut out the witty digressions and the clever ridicule of opponents, with which the reader was from time to time diverted.

Here then is Erasmus in a new aspect; proceeding to delight the world with his confidences and his humour, just as he charmed all with whom he came into personal contact. And from henceforward he draws all eyes upon him; until for the last twenty years of his life he was the primate of literary Europe, sought in company by kings and popes and cardinals, beloved by young and old.

Indications of his rising fame may be found in the books of this period. In August 1513, the famous Froben printed—entirely without permission, but such was the freedom of the printers to pirate each other's books—a reissue of the Aldine *Adagiorum Chiliades*. Just as it was being completed, Erasmus fell sick unto death in England, and rumour spread that he was gone. Froben, who had never met him, caused one of the scholars who worked for him to express world-wide regrets on the title-page of the new edition. The passage opens with a sentence adapted from Erasmus' own lament over Philip the Fair, and continues: 'What a grievous loss to good learning is this great man! He would have brought lustre not only to his native Germany' (of which Holland was then thought to form part) 'but to the whole of Europe; and would have edited many authors, who must now continue their struggle with the corruptions of worm and moth'—words which were echoed by Spiegel, an under-secretary in the Imperial Chancery, in a book printed at Vienna six months later.

The position he had gained may be read in two letters
which he wrote in 1514 and 1518, defending the way of
life that he had chosen for himself—to serve God by
advancing knowledge. The stricter members of his Order
objected to the freedom of his living, as he wandered
hither and thither, never in one stay. In the earlier letter
he was afraid that pressure might compel him to return
to Steyn, and shut off opportunities of doing the work to
which he had dedicated himself. He writes gravely to
his prior, Servatius Rogerus, of Rotterdam, an old friend
in whom he had confidence.

'Invitations come to me from Spain, from Italy, from France
and Germany, from England and Scotland: at Rome four of the
greatest cardinals and the present Pope treated me as a brother.
In England the King is most affectionate to me, the Queen
wished me to teach her. The Archbishops of Canterbury and
York load me with gifts and promises, and there is not a bishop
but would have me share his palace. The two universities compete to secure me; Lord Mountjoy, my former pupil, gives me
a yearly pension; the Dean of St. Paul's, John Colet, prefers my
society to that of any other companion.'

In 1518 his fears had been dispelled. The Pope had
given him a dispensation to go on with his work in his
own way; so he writes in a lighter vein, but with no less
honour awaiting him, if he would but take it.

'If I had wished, I might have gone to Spain in the train of
the Catholic King. The King of France offers me mountains of
gold. The King of England and the Cardinal of York invite me
with every kindness: so too the late Archbishop of Toledo, the
Bishop of Paris and the Bishop of Bayeux, the Archbishop of
Mainz, the Bishop of Liège, the Bishop of Utrecht, the Bishop
of Basle, the Bishop of Rochester, the Duke of Bavaria, the
Duke of Saxony. All these chances I have cast aside, preferring
to finish what I have in hand, the fruit of my long vigils. For
this perseverance my enemies call me inconstant. If constancy

means to stay the longest while in the same place, then we must give the highest praise to rocks and the trunks of trees, the next to shells and sponges. They would like me, I suppose, to have spent forty-five years soaking with them at the same board; though they too know how to bestir themselves, when they sight a bright fireside and catch delicious whiffs from the kitchen.'

After Erasmus moved off from the Netherlands in 1521, there was no cessation from these flattering proposals. Successive Popes, Adrian VI, his own countryman, and Clement VII, bade him come to Rome; Paul III wished to make him a Cardinal. The most Christian King again invited him to France; adding what was a most unusual honour, a few words in his own hand, 'Je vous auertys que sy vous voules venyr, que vous seres le byen venu. Françoys'. The letter may still be seen at Basle, the King's large handwriting scrawled boldly below the neat lines of his secretary. Margaret of Austria put on the pressure of withholding Erasmus' Imperial pension in order to bring him back to Brabant. In 1527 Henry VIII made another effort to draw him over to England. In 1528 the victorious King of Poland wrote 'Your letter' (of congratulation on the defeat of the Tartars) 'will win me credit throughout the world. How gladly would I repay such generosity, especially if we could only tempt you to come to us! But your friends tell me other princes have entreated you in vain; so no doubt I too shall be unsuccessful.' Even when Erasmus fled from Basle before the religious innovations which he mistrusted, and was uncertain where to find shelter for his last years, he would not surrender his freedom. Honours and wealth awaited him on every side: all that he would accept was a loan, which later proved to be a lease, of an empty house at Freiburg near by, which had been begun as a palace for Maximilian, and

which in its unfinished state Ferdinand had never cared
to use.

Besides these opportunities so resolutely set aside,
compliments flowed in upon him and gifts and money.
Bishops and legates came to Basle to see him, even for
an hour or two's conversation. The Bishop of Breslau
sent him sables and sand-clocks and nuggets of gold; a
brother, the Bishop of Olmütz, gold cups and Roman
coins. From the Archbishop of Canterbury came horses
for him to ride; from nuns at Cologne a yearly present of
sweetmeats. Spoons and forks (the new invention) of
gold and silver, bowls and drinking cups, rings with gems
and cameos, medals of reigning dukes and kings, choice
specimens of contemporary gold coins, fine linen from
Hungary, ermines from Poland, fish from the Lake of
Constance—all these came in a flood to testify the devotion of admirers in many lands.

It must be remembered that it was the fashion then
among kings and princes to 'collect' tame scholars for the
ornament of their courts; much as Frederick William the
First collected tall guardsmen, or young people to-day
collect birds' eggs or butterflies. Leonardo da Vinci, for
instance, spent his last years with Francis I. But even so,
it was surely a wonderful position for the friendless young
canon to have won for himself, after twenty years of
battling with the world. From the friends who lived in
his heart he received a homage which was little short of
adoration. To Thomas More he was 'Erasmus my dar-
ling', to the crusty lawyer Zasius he is usually 'Magnus
Erasmus' or 'Ter maximus'. In his sojourns at Basle he
attached to himself two of the sincerest friends that ever
man had, Beatus Rhenanus of Schlettstadt, and Boniface, the attractive young son of Froben's partner,
John Amorbach; men who would not have given their

whole-hearted devotion, except where it was most justly due.

The letters which reached him overflow with homage; but obviously *they* require some discounting. A surer indication of his place in the world may be found in a letter of Beatus Rhenanus to Zwingli, at Zurich, written from Schlettstadt, in January 1520, when Erasmus was far away in Louvain, out of any possibility that he might see the writer's actual words.

'Sapidus tells me that Leo Jud said here at a banquet, that Erasmus ought to be advised to make honourable mention in something that he writes, of the Abbot (of Einsiedeln, a member of the powerful family of Geroldseck). It seems to me that Leo does not properly understand how great Erasmus is; he thinks perhaps that he is just one of us. Erasmus is not to be measured by common standards; he has risen far above the summit of human greatness. You might suggest to the Abbot that he should give Erasmus cause by some present, say a cup worth thirty or forty gold pieces with an inscription in large letters "Presented to Erasmus, the parent of good learning, by Theobald of Geroldseck, abbot, 1520", or something of that sort. The money will not be lost; and don't let him be so scrupulous, or rather so superstitious, as to be afraid of the Virgin's anger if he spends a little of her property in this way: she likes good men to be treated well. If you agree that a silver cup should be sent, I should advise you to have it wrapped up in a case and sent to Basle, where it can be packed with the new edition of Cyprian which will be finished soon; and then a messenger engaged at the Abbot's expense can carry them both to Erasmus. Concealed in this way in paper, the cup will elude the brigands, of whom the country round Cologne is full. Perhaps, too, Froben will pay half the messenger's charge, so as to be able to write to Erasmus about his own affairs, and to get something brought back for him to print.'

Another incident, which Erasmus himself relates in describing a journey down the Rhine by boat in

September 1518, shows his credit in quite different circles.

'When we put in to Boppard' (which was the customs frontier between the Emperor and the Archbishop of Trèves), 'while the vessel was being examined, I went for a stroll on the bank. Someone recognized me, and pointed me out to the customs-official, a certain Christopher Eschenfelder. He was overjoyed, took me into his house, where some of my books were lying on the table among his office papers, and called to his wife and children and all his friends to tell them the good news. When the sailors began to cry out that they must be getting on, he sent them two bottles of wine, and two more again later; promising that he would let them off paying tolls on their return for having brought him such a visitor.'

To Eschenfelder himself, Erasmus wrote a lively letter of thanks on reaching his journey's end, Louvain:

'What a delightful surprise, to find such a friend at Boppard! a customs-officer who cares for the Muses and good learning! Christ reproached the Pharisees, saying that the publicans and harlots should go before them into the kingdom of heaven. What a disgrace it is to priests and monks! they live in ease and luxury, while officials spend their time in study; all *their* thoughts are of what they shall eat and what they shall drink, while Eschenfelder divides his hours between his Imperial Majesty and his books. It was easy to see what an idea you had formed of me beforehand; I am lucky if the sight of me has not spoiled your dream. That red wine of yours found favour with the captain's wife, a great bouncing woman with a fine thirst. She gulped it down, and would give no one else a chance. This made her quarrelsome, and she nearly slew her servant-girl with a big spoon; then going up on deck, she attacked her husband and almost toppled him into the Rhine. That's what comes of your wine!'

Eschenfelder never forgot this visit. Any friends of Erasmus who passed through Boppard received complimentary attentions at his hands. So long as the Master lived, they continued to correspond; and one of Erasmus' last compositions, *De puritate Ecclesiae*, is dedicated to this studious revenue-officer.

In all his later life, whenever Erasmus went on a journey, he was greeted in the cities where he halted with the honorific presents usually reserved for princes and ambassadors; casks of wine for himself and his friends, and sacks of oats for the horses; while crowds of admirers flocked to consume his leisure and exhaust him with fatigue. When he stayed with Botzheim at Constance, in September 1522, the succession of banquets and entertainments, even though relieved by quiet hours in the Cathedral library, was almost regal. At the end, in hope of inducing him to come again, his friend had his house pulled about, and replaced a stove with the open fire-place which Erasmus could not do without. At Freiburg, in March 1523, the magistrates sent the usual offerings to his inn, the Ship, and the University voted him a silver cup. In April 1524 he paid a surprise visit, incognito, to the Archdeacon of Besançon, Ferry Carondelet. His host was away, at his abbey of Montbenoît, and could not be got back in time. But dwelling in his house, Erasmus was quickly discovered by swarms of officious callers. After a few days the round of feasting was too much for him, and he kept his room for the remainder of his stay; even so the choirs of the churches came and sang to him underneath his window. By starting early he tried to slip away unobserved on his homeward journey to Basle.

'As I came out of my bedroom,' he tells us, 'there were three or four waiting on the landing to salute me, one of them a Franciscan. I mounted and rode out of the house-gate: in the street were several others, including the Dean of Montbéliard. As I passed the house of the Archbishop's Official, he was there on his mule and with him the Treasurer. Though I begged them to spare themselves the trouble, they rode with me all through the town and two miles outside. I was mounted on a comfortable nag, but not much to look at. The Official entreated me to change on to his mule, and to take his servant with me to Basle to bring it back. I had the utmost difficulty in declining.'

In 1528 a young Pole of good family, Andrew Zebrzy-dowski, spent a few months in Erasmus' household, learning eagerly from the Master's lips. When he died as Bishop of Cracow, in 1560, he had inscribed upon his tomb that he had been 'magni illius Erasmi discipulus et auditor'.

What was the secret of the remarkable ascendancy which Erasmus held over his world, and after four centuries holds in some measure still? It may be found in the combination of brilliant intellectual gifts with absolute sincerity and enduring purpose. As a thinker he was not perhaps profound: he had lived too much with his books, and had not experience enough of mankind at large to deal with all the problems on which he was invited to pronounce. His strength lay rather in the power to grasp important truths and to present them with cogency in spontaneous, irresistible eloquence; never succumbing to the temptations which beset many brilliant minds, to pursue novelty and paradox at the cost of making the better appear the worse, and, for fear of cant, to bespatter in their mirth the high things they really venerate. His retentive memory and his ability to work almost, it seemed, without ceasing, gave him a vast store of erudition. By steady practice in his earlier years and a natural insight into the use of language, he acquired a style which, while free and flexible and consummately lucid, could always command force and weight to give strength to its graceful charm. Added to this was a keen sense of humour, and a wit which in its moments of plainest speaking never failed of delicacy—a point in which he was in marked advance of his contemporaries. In an age when the art of writing Latin was highly valued, when elegance could cover and condone mountains of the most tedious platitudes, a man who could write Latin more quickly and more surely than most people write their own language was bound to win admiration.

It is interesting to compare the rough-drafts of Erasmus' letters with those of his correspondents. Theirs for the most part show unmistakable signs of painful composition and repeated correction: words scratched through and transferred elsewhere, and then perhaps scratched through again and brought back to their original place: sentences begun several times over, with slight variations of form: the whole document so botched that it is difficult to concoct a connected sense; and often so when the theme is merely an accumulation of stiff compliments and musty commonplaces. With Erasmus it is quite different. However important his subject, whether he is corresponding with principalities or powers, whether he is discussing fine points of scholarship, or, in answer to virulent attacks, defining his own position with nice care, the lines flow swiftly over the page, true and even, with hardly a word corrected, unless it be some mis-writing, the outcome of haste. Occasionally he strikes out a whole passage with which he is dissatisfied, and goes on again, the stream of thought unbroken by the check. Even if, as sometimes, he loses the thread of his argument or gets entwined by its sudden turns, he disentangles himself with neatness, leaving the reader scarcely aware that any new idea has broken in to perturb his even progress. Here and there his writing is so rapid that his secretary could not decipher it, and marked words to be asked when the fair copy was being made for dispatch. 'Most of my books have been written headlong; this is a real fault of my nature', he confessed to Adrian VI. Elsewhere he writes, 'What I have once begun, I like to finish almost without a break. I cannot bear the slow task of correction.' Or again, 'I did not mean to let anything of this come in; but my mind said one thing and my pen wrote another.' In the printing-house he would race with the compositors, to see whether he could not turn out copy faster than they could set up the type; and many of his controversial works are veritable *tours de force*, dashed off in the few days' interval between the arrival of some new attack upon him and the departure of the printers for the Frankfort fair—a half-yearly festival which must not be missed, or else his critic would have held the field, unanswered, for six months.

This headlong trait in his character shows itself in many ways. About figures, especially dates, he is often incorrect, though sometimes with a show of precision: 'twenty-three years ago, unless I am mistaken', when he should have said nineteen; 'nearly thirty', when he means twenty-two. Men's Christian names he frequently has wrong: Cardinal Caietano appears as Jacobus instead of Thomas; the famous Pastor of Groningen, William Frederiks, is styled Peter in the first edition; Zwingli, with whom for some time he was intimate, is addressed in an autograph letter as John instead of Ulrich. If taxed with inaccuracy, he would not have questioned the justice of the complaint, and he would have done his best to avoid it in the future; only he could not stay to get these small things right. His pen rushed on, striving to keep pace with the thoughts bubbling up in his mind, as he stood at his desk; and there was no time to halt for verification of details.

His concentration upon his high purposes may be seen in another matter which has had important consequences affecting the judgement of posterity upon him. The publication of letters was a form of literary exhibition which public opinion recognized as permissible to men of acknowledged eminence; and after the introduction of printing a few such volumes appeared, their contents mostly chosen as specimens of ornate and pompous elegance, triumphs of the art of saying very little in a great many words. They were printed for the most part from the rough-drafts which the writer had composed first, to be copied fair before being sent off; and which were kept both for convenience of reference when, perhaps months later, an answer came back, and from reluctance to part with compositions which had cost much effort, and which the writer presumably admired.

As early as 1506, when he was little more to the world than *vn frère augustin*, Erasmus was taking steps to preserve his letters; even inquiring from some of his earliest friends whether they had kept those they had received from him and could return them. But he did not venture to publish anything in this kind till 1515, and then only a few of distinction addressed to the Pope and Cardinals, and tacked on to a volume of compositions by others. In 1516 came a thin volume of letters, a large number of which were written to him, not by him. Another again in 1517, and a fuller volume in 1518. By this time he was in his stride. He had made his name, his means were roughly adequate to his needs, and he could not stop to ponder over trifles. His friends at Basle asked for more *Epistolae*, to be published for the delight of the world of letters. Erasmus' reply was to send them sheaves of his rough-drafts, and leave them free to print what they liked.

This was the origin of his *Farrago*, a collection containing many of his early letters written in Paris and Tournehem and Oxford, at St. Omer and Cambridge and London, with two even which go back to his monastic days at Steyn, thirty years before. The book was printed at Basle in 1519, while Erasmus was at Louvain; we need not suppose that he ever saw the proofs or took any part in the production. When it came to a new edition, enlarged by half its size, in 1521, Erasmus cut out or softened down a few passages which he considered indiscreet, or put in pseudonyms in remarks about his friends which he thought were likely to wound; but otherwise the book came out unchanged. So we may fairly assume that he ratified what his editor friends had done; only he would not spend his own time on such work.

His indifference may be shown again by his attitude to the big collection of his letters, *Opus Epistolarum*, which came out in 1529, comprising all the volumes which had appeared before. A friend had urged him to arrange them in order of time, so that they might be read with some continuity. This was too much for him to undertake; but he looked through the *Farrago* and put in a number of year-dates, which had not been recorded on the rough-drafts, and which therefore the editors of 1519 had not been able to supply. Out of 200 which he added in this way, more than half are demonstrably wrong. It was a matter of no consequence to him. He did what he could to please a friend; but he had no time to spare for attaining precision.

In these later volumes Erasmus, perhaps almost without knowing it, had created for his own age a new kind in literature. In place of the earlier monuments of elegance, he offered to the world, for its light reading, a real medley of letters, grave and gay, more familiar than anything which had appeared since Cicero; many of them on trifling subjects, but showing the master hand in their crisp reality, focusing attention on the points of interest, and lighting up so vividly the course of everyday life as to close up for us the centuries and show how little human nature varies from itself as the ages go by. It is a kind for which the Dutch seem to have a special gift. There is the same touch, the vivid portrayal of ordinary life, in those little biographic sketches of the brethren who surrounded Gerard Groot or Florence Radewijns, or in de Voecht's Chronicle of the House of the Brethren at Zwolle. And through all these volumes of his Letters runs the vein of expansive self-revelation which we noticed in the *Adagiorum Chiliades*.

Here then is one reason why so much interest is felt in Erasmus, that we know so much about him. Men of action, even when they find a 'vates sacer', go to their graves quickly, and then all their thoughts perish. Great warriors like Roland or Bayard are known to us mainly from the outside. Their brave deeds in the high places of the field become the themes of song and romance; but if we would know what manner of men they were in their goings out and comings in and in all the plain relations of human life, we have little beyond our imaginations with which to fill in the details. With kings and states-men and law-givers there is the same lack, so long as we must estimate them only from their achievements. The character of any act depends very largely on the spirit in which it is done; and if we can go no further than the knowledge that it has been done, we are left to divine for ourselves the spirit which moved it; and such divinations vary with the taste of the diviner. In a lesser degree it is the same even with men of art and letters, divines and philosophers, and those whose lives are cast among books. The case of Shakespeare shows that a man's writings may be known through all the world, and yet his personality remain obscure and impenetrable.

In his familiar letters Erasmus is revealed to us as few others of his own or earlier periods ever have been. His character was not free from blemishes; such is the way of men. Besides his high and noble gifts there were the defects of his qualities. The intense fervour with which he gave himself to his work carried him very much into the centre of his own picture, and made it difficult for him to see that things might appear differently to others. The little needle of his tongue flashed out and pierced the joints of men's harness, while he was quite unconscious of their smart. 'I cannot understand', he wrote, 'why some people so dislike me. I have never written a line to blacken any man's fame.' Again, with his ardent impulsive nature it was not easy for him to practise reserve. What he thought, he said; what he felt, came bursting out, and was as quickly forgotten, by him, if not by others. It is easy therefore to convict him of many unpleasing faults, by quoting against him his own words. And any one who thinks that Luther was a fine fellow— as indeed he was—has no difficulty in disparaging the character of one who was frequently in combat with the great Reformer.

It is important to notice that on many of these charges Erasmus is the chief, indeed practically the only, witness against himself. It is almost entirely on evidence supplied in his *Farrago* of 1519 that are based the charges of selfish *exigence* to the faithful Batt, of ingratitude to the Bishop of Cambray, even while eating his bread at Paris, of flattering the Lady of Veere to her face while

mocking her behind her back, of timidity in times of
danger, of equivocation in denying the authorship of
books which might get him into trouble. The fact is that
though Erasmus knew how to be discreetly reticent when
prudence really required it, or how to propitiate with
smooth words the patrons who could help him in his
work, he rarely paused to consider what the world in
general was thinking about him, how his actions would
seem or his words would sound. There was, as we say,
'no humbug about him'; he did not pretend to be what
he was not. Conscious of great aims and giving all his
power to serve them, he would not waste a thought on
'keeping up appearances', except in so far as a good
report among men might promote the success of his
enterprises. So when his friends asked for more Letters
to publish, he gave them what he saw would amuse the
public; without troubling to think that careful busy-
bodies might lay sentence to sentence and piece up a
calumny.

I have said nothing about the religious controversies
which cast a shadow over Erasmus' later years. They
were very real, upon live issues; and they stirred men
quickly to be faithful unto death for what they thought
to be right, and bitter unto persecution of those they
thought to be wrong. But to Erasmus, nothing was more
distasteful than controversy. For the speculative pursuit
of truth he saw that the prime requisites were freedom
from heat and passion, freedom from any desire to van-
quish an adversary. His instinct was to lay stress upon
the points on which men agree, and to postpone decision
where there are differences. So long as he could, he refused to measure pens with Luther, knowing that they
agreed in much that was good; and when at length he
was driven and coaxed into the field, he chose a subject—

the effect of Luther's doctrine of Grace upon the conception of the Freedom of man's Will—which, while penetrating to the centre of Luther's position, was not one to kindle emotion, or to admit of settlement before the tribunal of popular opinion. Even so the extremists of both sides raged against him because he was not with them; the moderates, on the contrary, looked to him as the one hope of Christianity and the Church. But to him it was lost time. The light that shone ever before his eyes, leading him on, was the brightness of knowledge; in quest of this he would expend every effort and make every sacrifice, hoping for real progress. But to triumph over men with no more light than himself seemed to him a barren victory, and he had no wish for it: though when once launched upon a controversy, he became as other disputants. The study of the Bible and the Fathers held out the best hopes of bringing him nearer to the light he sought: he plunged into it and grudged everything that turned him from it. Not for himself he sought: what he found was to be the possession of all. Especially he rejoiced in exposition, his facile pen making the work a pleasure. His Paraphrases, which to him were a kind of commentary, giving him freedom to expand and to digress, were written with happy alacrity; 'Here', he said, 'I am on my own ground.'

But as to Socrates, knowledge to him was virtue; and in seeking knowledge he sought also the fruits of the spirit, peace and joy and the many facets of ordinary goodness which the Apostle enumerates. If Erasmus was happy in expounding the Scriptures, he was happy also in persuading men to virtue: to self-mastery and moderation, to the good manners which spring from real consideration for others, to high ideals of Christian marriage, to the pure affection which seeketh its neighbour's good.

And as in the sphere of speculation he minimized differences, so in the sphere of practical conduct he would reconcile the inevitable clash of individual interests by a spirit of compromise, which, seeking not its own, is more ready to give than to receive; and by a spirit of toleration which finds the best rather than the worst.

It was from this angle that he approached the religious conflicts of his day, reluctant to take part in them himself, and dreading their effect upon the harmonious growth of the cause to which he had devoted his life. It has been thought that the Reformation of the Church, which its own leaders knew to be urgently needed, might have come more easily and more successfully if the counsels of Erasmus could have prevailed over the counsels of Luther. With many of the faults that required correction, the grosser things which men's consciences permit but which none can defend, this might very likely have been so; but it may be questioned whether sharper measures than Erasmus would have admitted were not necessary for those 'fond things vainly invented', the tender and beautiful phantasies which cling round religion like ivy embracing an old building, and whose champions are to be found among the blameless and the true of heart—real superstitions, surviving into ages beyond their own.

It is interesting too to speculate whither Erasmus' principles would have led him. With all his outspoken criticism of the Church, his piercing satire which found out the weak spots and showed them up to the ridicule of the public, he remained a loyal Churchman to the end. Yet it may be asked—Whither would he have journeyed in his unflinching quest of truth? How would the foundations of his life have appeared as the light that he sought grew stronger before him? Again, with all his heart he hated schism, and his conservative temperament dreaded disorder; yet he would perhaps have judged Luther differently and feared him less, if he could have foreseen the success of the Lutherans in erecting, amid what seemed like chaos, an ordered Church, standing firm through the centuries upon its quickly-laid foundations, and upholding those simple virtues which are the common treasure of all good men.

These are some of the considerations which may help us to answer the second of our questions—Why are people so interested in Erasmus? History unrolls before us a list, stretching far back out of sight, of men who have had gifts as great as his, and purposes as high, and of whom we are yet content to know not very much, because they do not quicken our interest. But how often has such a combination of talents as had Erasmus been found in one man? He has many sides, to win sympathy; and whatever subject he touches, he illuminates. The scholar, the theologian, the grammarian, all recognize the importance of his work, even though it may now be out of date, or where they may not agree with it; the historian turns over his pages with delight, never knowing what he may not find; for the student of education or of morals there is much that is directly important; the peacemakers reprint his exhortations in that great cause from generation to generation; lovers of literature find his lighter works ever new. And for those who are interested in human nature—and who is not?—there is a gallery of characters, almost as rich as in Theophrastus or in Earle: the bright schoolboy, the reluctant canon, the poor student, the brilliant friend, the horseman, the gay courtier, the anxious traveller, the matchless scholar, courted and besought of kings, yet holding them all at arm's length; finally the Master lapped in the devotion of his followers, toiling daily with them in his 'mill', now exacting and imperious, laying on them burdens heavy as his own, now charming them with natural, unforced merriment. It is this wonderful combination which has placed him where he stands. His intensely human temperament kept him from the pedestal of Bernard; his wide sympathies from the stern convictions of Zwingli or Calvin. His sense of humour preserved him from domineering with Luther; his delicacy from rollicking in the mud with Rabelais; his sincerity saved him from the withering bitterness of Voltaire. Above all he could not be dull.

If one reflects on the length and permanence of tradition, it is tempting to ask how far the interest in Erasmus is due to remembrance of what he was. We have seen what he did with his ready pen; we need not doubt that he was equally ready with his tongue. In a company of talkers there is usually some one who takes the lead, whose pre-eminence once established is conceded without a struggle by others who are content to listen to what they cannot emulate. This leadership is awarded to the highest combination of gifts, brilliance and readiness, wit and power to amuse, fearlessness and good taste, sympathy to understand what is passing through the minds of those who sit round. From the testimony of those who knew Erasmus, it seems that wherever he went, in whatever company he found himself, he could, if he wished, assume control of the conversation and enthral his listeners.

We have seen what his contemporaries said of him to one another. Tradition of such leadership may well last long. Here is an utterance about him in the next generation. In 1553, Froben's grandson, Nicholas Episcopius, published the first book he printed, an edition of Politian, with a dedication to Charles Harst, an official

in the Duke of Cleve's service and formerly an inmate
of Erasmus' house at Basle. He reminds Harst of the
friendship formed with Episcopius' parents and the
Froben family in the days 'when for the sake of our
Erasmus, a man worthy of everlasting remembrance,
this country of ours was visited by learned and honourable men, whom he attracted as the magnet does the iron,
by an invisible sympathy and by similarity of studies,
in which he was without rival'. Episcopius, who wrote
this, when Erasmus died was only a boy of five; so that
he was not recalling his own experience. The seventeen
years which had elapsed seem comparatively a brief
space; but in the ceaseless procession of human life new
faces are always jostling out the old, and in fact the names
of men who died seventeen years ago, though they may
be often in our hearts, are not often on our lips. After
only half a generation there are many to whom it is use-
less to speak of them. So tradition was already strong.

There have been other things to keep Erasmus' name
alive. At Basle his benefaction for poor students is ad-
ministered to this day. Rotterdam has its Erasmiaansch
Gymnasium. One of our great schools, Christ's Hospital,
has two forms in which long ago his books were read,
known still as Great Erasmus and Little Erasmus. 'Ad
insigne Erasmi' has been a favourite sign for booksellers and printers and publishers. He is indissolubly
connected with the Western pronunciation of Greek.
Through England and Wales, by ordinance of Edward VI
and Elizabeth, translations of his Paraphrases were
placed in every parish church. It is perhaps a consequence of this that in Cardiganshire his name is synony-
mous with a wise or learned man, 'Rasmws o ddyn'.

Yet it may not be altogether fanciful to think that
what makes men still interested in him is not this fre-

quent use of his name, but some half-conscious remembrance, repeated from one age to another, of the Master
of those who talk, the tireless seeker after knowledge, the
brave merry heart, never daunted, never at a loss, always
fascinating, always true, *vbique certe* ἐράσμιος, *hoc est
amabilis*, as Beatus Rhenanus says in concluding his
biography. If this fancy has any foundation, there may
be truth in the words which John Colet wrote to him in
1516, when the New Testament was completed, *Nomen
Erasmi nunquam peribit*.

to p. 40

ERASMUS' SERVICES TO LEARNING

THERE are epochs in the world's history when a material invention suddenly opens up great and undreamed of possibilities. In the nineteenth century railways and the electric telegraph evidently improved communications: insensibly they made the government of the world more effective, and gave to the individual a degree of security such as he had never before enjoyed. In the present generation the invention of the motor for engineering purposes almost in a moment made it possible to fly. Similarly in the fifteenth century the invention of printing enabled Western scholars to make great and rapid advances into the field of exact learning, such as since Alexandrian days they had been unable to imagine. The age of manuscripts gave way slowly to the age of printed books; but the humanists were not slow to perceive that a new instrument had been placed in their hands with which to wage what Solomon calls the Great War of Ignorance.

It is not possible to determine when or where printing began in the West, any more than we can say to-day when and by whom the telephone or wireless telegraphy were invented. For so striking a result the preparatory labour of many heads is required. In China block-printing has been traced back to the eighth century, in Japan to the twelfth: in 1403 an emperor of Corea was casting movable types of copper. With caravan communication so well established that delicate Chinese porcelain could find its way to European markets in the fifteenth century, it seems probable that news of the Eastern invention must have come through, and set men to work to imitate. The Dutch claim the discovery for Coster at Haarlem, the Germans with more acceptance for Gutenberg at Mainz. But it is enough for our purpose to know that in Europe the first printed book to which can be assigned a definite date—Gutenberg's Latin Bible—was completed by 1456. Ten years or so later—he himself was not sure of his age, so that it is not for us to be precise— Erasmus was born into this new world of great possibilities; where, after a long struggle against friendlessness and lack of opportunity, at the age of forty-five he won his freedom, freedom to work as he chose and to devote himself to the promotion of Christian learning. That was his life's work: his high achievement is not always recognized as it deserves.

With his brilliant talents and his quick sympathies he could not stand aloof from men. He must learn from them, and he must lead. Now and again he made excursions into politics, pouring out some rapid disquisition on troubles in Church and State; or using his keen wit and humour to make men laugh at the follies of the time. So he entered into the conflicts of the day; and to wide circles he became either the man whose eyes were open or the dangerous critic who must at all costs be crushed. But his real victories were won in his study and in the printing-house. There, captaining a band of scholars whom he fired with his own enthusiasm, he spent his ripe years on illumining those realms of oblivion into which the world is daily being carried by the passage of ineluctable Time.

The invention of printing made it possible to multiply books sixtyfold, an hundredfold, a thousandfold. This was its first and evident advantage: simultaneously it gave to scholars the power of co-operation. It requires an effort of thought to realize with what difficulty men worked when they had only manuscripts. No two manuscripts could be identical page for page without great trouble taken; and that such trouble was not taken is shown by the method invented in the thirteenth century for identifying manuscripts in the catalogues of libraries. A modern catalogue distinguishes books by the date and place of their printing: the medieval librarian, having no such obvious means, marked the books by the first words of the second leaf. The first words of the first leaf were the opening words of the treatise, whatever it was, and therefore were always the same: his use of those of the second leaf implies that no attempt was made by scribes to follow the pages of their originals. It was not to the tenth or the twentieth leaf that he need turn for some sure divergence to be reached: by the second leaf already the scribe had certainly begun to diverge—the size of his page probably constituting a fundamental difference—and the method of distinction was therefore sure.

With all manuscripts unlike, a scholar might number the pages of his own, but he could not refer from these to the manuscript of a friend. Here printing brought an improvement. Every page of a book was identical with the corresponding page in every copy of the same edition; and a man might direct a friend to a page and even a line, which was at once to be found. Yet this advantage was not at first perceived. The early printers 'signed' their pages by quires, as the scribes had written them. At first the signature was put only at the extreme corner of the page, for the use of the binder, who was instructed to shear them off, and usually did so. So placed they may be seen in large copies of the Strasburg Vincent of Beauvais, 1473. Later, when their convenience for the reader was noticed, they were advanced to the foot of the type.

The first person to whom it occurred to number the

leaves of a book was the Cologne printer, Arnold ter Hoernen who, in printing a sermon delivered in 1470, put numbers not at the top corners, but in the middle of the right-hand margins of the rectos.[1] His example was, not quickly followed. The method of signatures was more familiar to the masters of medieval book-craft; and so they remained for some years as the only means of distinguishing pages. The St. Albans printer of the *Chronicles of England, c.* 1485, is at pains to point out how useful they are for the construction of an index. 'You must understand that every leaf is marked under with A one, two, three, and four, and so forth to eight, all the letters; and whatsome ever you find shortly written in this table, you shall find openly in the same letter.'

Another sign of the want of co-operation among scholars is the long time that elapsed before literature was divided into small sections for convenience of reference. Voluminous authors, Livy for instance, cut up their works into books from the beginning; but the chapters are only found in editions of the seventeenth century, the sections are quite modern. Until printing came it was of no avail to make small divisions. There was no means of securing acceptance of any one system of division; and to have a number of systems, each different from the rest, was worse than to have none at all. Even the Bible, the object of so much study, had no chapters till Stephen Langton made them in the thirteenth century; the verses it was left for Robert Stephanus to divide and number—the Psalms, from their use in Church, had been divided into verses, though unnumbered, long before—as he fled from Paris to Geneva, when branded with heresy in 1554. The medieval scholar was content

---

[1] For this information I am obliged to Prof. A. W. Pollard.

to cite authors by their names, *vt ait Tullius, quod scribit Fabius*; sometimes only *vt ait ille*, if he was not sure of the ascription. He can perhaps give the number of a book of Pliny or of a letter of Jerome; but that is the utmost.

A curious exception is in the works of the fifteenth-century publicist, John Gerson, who acquired fame during the Council of Constance. They were so much in use that a system was devised of numbering them by alphabets, for example, Alphabet 46, letter Z, or Alphabet 87, letter M, each letter denoting about thirty lines of matter; and this cumbrous method survived in use as late as 1525, although a splendid printed edition, with each leaf clearly numbered, had appeared in Paris four years before.

The lack of co-operation is shown in another way. In the earliest printed books it is rare to find any indication of the manuscripts used. Sweynheym and Pannartz plunge at once into the matter in hand. The author appears on the very first page; often there is no title, no preface, no table of contents, no introductory verses. Even at the end the colophon is of the barest. Usually the book consists of the author and nothing more. With Jenson's Plutarch it is just the same; indeed one may read through the whole series of prefaces to the *editiones principes* of the classics in the compilation of the magnificent Beriah Botfield, and find no mention of the manuscripts employed, until after the turn of the sixteenth century. The Aldine prefaces are full of graceful compliments to patrons, of praise of the author, of remarks on the importance of classical studies; but it is exceptional to find anything about the sources.

In this silence the early printers were no doubt following the custom of the makers of manuscripts, and reflecting their outlook. Each manuscript was an individual

thing, written for sale to others or for a man's own use;
as Rudolph Agricola copied out Homer when teaching
himself Greek. In either case the mention of the source
was unimportant. To the writer it was known, and there
was no need to record it; a purchaser was too happy in
the treasure he had acquired to wish to find any fault
in it, certainly not to question its ancestry. To scholars
of to-day intent upon the Tradition and laboriously
affiliating manuscripts by study of various readings, a
brief colophon recording the sources from which a manuscript had been copied would be invaluable. Pious ejacu-
lations by weary scribes rejoicing in the completion of
their toil are sometimes found: dates of time and place
are rare. Even when these are clearly stated in long
colophons, by John Serbopoulos of Constantinople copying manuscripts at Reading, presumably in the Abbey,
in 1499 and 1500, he does not think to tell us what were
the originals before him. Were they his own, carried
about with him as matrices from which to cast others?
or did the Abbot bring them forth from his treasure to
be copied by the wandering Greek? Serbopoulos' completion of the Corpus Suidas, begun by his countryman
Emmanuel who was many years his senior, suggests that
the latter view may be right.

How slowly dawned upon the minds of scholars the
idea that later generations would be interested in the
sources of their work may be shown from a single example: Augustine's *City of God*, a treatise which enjoyed
remarkable popularity in the fifteenth century. Sweynheym and Pannartz printed it three times between 1465
and 1470, and twenty-four editions are known before
1496. Yet the first to give any indication of the manuscripts used is Froben's of 1522, which Vives edited under
the supervision of Erasmus. The practice, when once

introduced, grew rapidly. Later in the sixteenth century a printer or editor producing any text newly discovered would have been ashamed to leave unpraised the name of the friend who had communicated the manuscript to him; and often precise details are given as to where it had been found.

This indifference to manuscripts when once they had been copied or printed, this sense that they would not be needed because no one troubled about the source of the text before him, appears in another way. Erasmus records that generous owners in their enthusiasm for the spread of learning by printing would send manuscripts to Aldus from all parts of Europe and never expect to see them again: adding, however, that not all owners were generous, and that some erred on the side of caution, allowing no one to set eyes on their treasures. For the second edition of his New Testament he borrowed two Greek manuscripts from the Austin priory at Corsendonk. When returning them he inscribed on one of them 'Seruetur', on the other φυλαχθήτω, words which convey ominous suggestion of what might be expected to happen to manuscripts which had once been used for the press.

Through the power of co-operation the printer's art gave to the world the conception of standard texts, which in the days of manuscripts many factors had combined to counteract. An author whose work, though first-rate, was not for the wide public, would probably not resort to manuscript production on a large scale. He might perhaps multiply his book, as Caxton did with his *Histories of Troy*, by copying it out a few times with his own hand; or if he paid others to write copies for him, he would no doubt collate and correct them himself out of compliment to those to whom they were to be presented. Either process invited to variation of the text.

As he rewrote what he had composed, at every point it was open to him to write it otherwise. He was not deterred by loyalty to an original, the work of some one else. The book was his own, and wherever he judged that he could make it better, he naturally did so. Or if he was correcting a copy made by a hireling, there, too, there was a temptation to improve, even though at cost of some defacement of the page. Hence it might easily happen that with books of the first importance there were considerable variations in the copies in circulation, even though several of them were in the author's autograph. And when a generation had passed and the author was dead, it might be impossible to determine which was the best form of a book, which the first state, and which the text finally adopted. Bach's music, with its infinite variety of autograph manuscript authority, is a notable example of this in a later age.

Such a state of uncertainty and flux encouraged men to compilation. A work of literature, a play of Sophocles or a treatise by Cicero, would of course evoke respect as a product of genius, and therefore not to be tampered with. But anything designed to be helpful, a dictionary or an encyclopaedia, the commentary on Virgil which passes under the name of Servius, a chronicle or the *Liber Pontificalis*, would only be improved by additions —new words in an index, new references in a collection of notes, new records or biographies. Plagiarism, too, the transference of others' work into one's own, became easy. Literary criticism held that there was one way of stating a thing which was better than all others; and if the best way had been attained by some one else, there was no good in seeking after what was bound to be less good. If, therefore, authorship were uncertain, or there was no credit to be sought or gained, such transference of another's work might seem almost the natural thing. Literary forgery also flourished, a pursuit which sometimes has had attractions for persons otherwise intelligent. Hence great variety ensued in manuscripts and uncertainty in ascription of authorship: leading to confusion so soon as scholars began to plan printed editions, with the consequent obligation of marking off the false from the genuine. Hence, too, perhaps the slowness with which emerged the conception of ownership in literature and its protection by copyright.

Again, the world of manuscripts was difficult to explore. Vellum books were heavy to carry by land, and their shape inconvenient. Ships or barges offered more space; but the greedy sea was no respecter of Letters, and even rivers had rocks and rapids. In consequence it was not easy to lay one manuscript beside another and make a careful collation. The monasteries worked hard at this, taking great pains, especially with texts of divinity; but in spite of all their labours many manuscripts must have rusted, lying on the desks of libraries or packed away in the cupboards of private houses, seen by few eyes since the generation for which they were written. With so much unexamined material, the text of every book whose author was dead might be challenged as to its excellence, that is its nearness to the original, by every other copy in existence. And such a challenge could not lightly be disposed of. To collate two manuscripts together is not the work of a day. Only by close observation can it be discovered whether they are roughly the same, with no large insertions or omissions; verbal differences, small of space, but perhaps important in sense, can only be detected by word for word comparison from beginning to end. How easy it must have been for differences in manuscripts to escape unnoticed is shown by an Oxford undergraduate's discovery of thirty new lines of Juvenal slumbering in a Bodleian manuscript, four and a half centuries after scholars had begun to form and fix the text in print.

The advent of printing brought a new era. A printed book was at once a foundation for others to build upon; also the clear type made the work of collation quicker and surer, and thus invited to the task. The 275 or more copies of an edition dispersed throughout many libraries formed an archetype with which manuscripts might be collated as they were found, and their variants marked. Politian knew this very well: who, in his Rome Pliny, 1473, now in the Bodleian, records at the end, first that he completed his critical examination of the text for the purpose of his lectures on 15 August 1480, just when the Turks were ravaging Otranto, and secondly that by 1490 he had collated it three times, with two manuscripts borrowed from St. Mark's at Florence, and with a third lent by King Ferdinand (of Naples); and on the first leaf he mentions other manuscripts whose various readings he notes in the margins throughout the book.

Again, a library of printed books was easier to examine. Two manuscripts might be identical, word for word; but the fact could not be established without careful labour over many days. A man finding on his friend's shelves the Florentine Homer or the Aldine Aristotle knows at once that they are identical with his own.

Finally, printing brought permanence and the hope of long life, and therewith encouragement to take pains. A medieval scholar's work in editing some author of whom he was fond might end in no more than a single copy; unless he was prepared to give time to making

other copies himself or could afford to hire a scribe.
And a single manuscript is exposed to all the material
risks of fire and sword, of moth and rust that corrupt;
and not less fatal is oblivion. When a man dies, his
possessions pass to other hands. Gold and silver readily
find new owners. Land and houses will not lack feet to
walk proudly over them, for the day which in More's
fancy seems so short to Mother Earth who has known
many masters. But books, old papers, there are few to
want; and so manuscripts which had been the treasures
of some brilliant scholar, which, like Pico, 'he had with
great travail and watch compiled', might through mis-
fortune, the lack of natural heirs or of any one working
in the same field, to be concerned about them, disappear
and become palimpsests, or be cut into tailors' measures
or serve confectionaries for the wrappings of cakes.
Medieval houses were cramped, with few rooms of any
size except the hall. After fifty years the remains of
some author whose very name was almost forgotten
might easily be looked upon as encumbrances, rubbish
to be thrown away by those who have put up with it
too long.

Such were some of the conditions in the world of
learning when Erasmus was born. The prime need was
for standard editions to fix texts; not good and thorough
editions, but something to begin upon, and as soon as
possible—of course as good as they could be made—to
be emended and improved by the labour of later generations. At Rome a beginning was made with the literature of the Romans: from Germany came the first
editions of the Schoolmen: the Aldine firm supplied
them for the Greeks. Erasmus' life-work was to do this
for the New Testament and the Fathers: out of whose

writings he could not only elucidate the Gospels, but also correct their text.

At what date he framed, consciously or unconsciously, this scheme of work is not clear. To a man with his antecedents and upbringing his career was necessarily dependent upon opportunity. Unless he could open a way for himself, wherever he might decide that it was his duty to go, it might easily happen that his talents would lie buried. Within his monastery, as his letters show, he certainly had opportunities to read both the classics and the Fathers. When he made his way out to serve a bishop, further chances came to him. A friend who saw him at Groenendael, an Austin priory in the Forest of Soigne, marked how he wandered up and down the library, and at length picked up Augustine from the desk; and then, after diligent reading there, carried a volume off to his cell for such hours of light as the canonical night might afford. Others in the house laughed at such intensity: for them Augustine had no interest.

Even when his patron let him go to a university, the objects that he had in view are nowhere clearly expressed. Freedom to educate himself was no doubt foremost in his mind, and almost of necessity he read for a degree in theology. His letters from Paris to his Prior in Holland aver the desire to give himself wholly to sacred learning; but that was what was expected of him, and his protestations are therefore not entirely convincing, though they may well have been genuine enough. The first clear indication is in his correspondence during the Michaelmas Term that he spent at Oxford in 1499. With Colet, a few months his junior, he had had long talks; and when the time came for Erasmus to go, Colet sought to detain him. They agreed in revolt against the fantastic speculations then in fashion in the schools, and in demanding a more concrete and historical study of the Bible. The questions they would ask were, not how mankind would have been born if our first parents had not fallen, nor whether the wicked continue to sin in hell, but what were the words of Christ, and by what means these had been preserved to posterity. Colet had been treating the New Testament from this point of view; and he pressed Erasmus to stay and do the same by the Old. But the homeless and destitute scholar would not stay to enjoy comfort and friendship. Colet's method had raised the question of the Tradition, and Erasmus saw that it must be answered. If the Scriptures were to be treated historically, they must be studied in their original form, or in the nearest form to that, which critical scholarship could discover. 'When I feel that I have attained my proper strength, I will come to your side and do my best to maintain true theology.' The New Testament must be read in Greek, the Old in Hebrew: the former language Erasmus taught himself after disappointment with the only Greek teacher available in the West, George Hermonymus of Sparta; Hebrew he attempted, but never made much progress in it.

The tide of this impulse bore him swiftly along. In 1501, while staying with a patron in the great abbey of St. Omer, he wrote a treatise of moral exhortation and precept, *The Enchiridion of a Christian Soldier*, which is still highly praised. In its closing passage he declares his faith to the person he was addressing.

'Shun bad company, and make the Prophets, Christ, and the Apostles your friends. Above all, choose Paul. For long I have been labouring over a commentary upon him. A bold task this seems; but I follow Origen, Ambrose, Augustine, and many later theologians, and with God's help I trust that I do not labour in vain. I hope to disarm some critics who think it is the highest religion to know nothing of good learning. It was not for empty fame or childish pleasure that in my youth I grasped at the polite literature of the ancients, and by late hours gained some slight mastery of Greek and Latin. It has long been my cherished wish to cleanse the Lord's temple of barbarous ignorance, and to adorn it with treasures brought from afar, such as may kindle in generous hearts a warm love for the Scriptures.'

Three years later, when he was nearing forty and still dependent on such bounty as he could charm or wring from others, or on the precarious earnings of his pen, he renewed his relations with Colet. 'My sails are spread, and I am hastening after sacred learning as fast as the winds will carry me. I long to be at work upon it, and to throw aside the worldly tasks in which I am still involved. Soon I hope to extricate myself.' The letter led, as it was no doubt intended to do, to an invitation. Colet, as dean of St. Paul's, brought his friend back to London and gave him leisure. With the help of two old Latin manuscripts from the Cathedral Library, Erasmus made in about a year a new translation of the whole New Testament except Acts and Revelation; but as to the Greek manuscripts which he used he is provokingly silent. Then he seized a chance of going to Italy in quest of teachers and libraries, leaving the work behind to be copied by Colet's scribe, Peter Meghen.

In 1509 he returned, having completed his *Adagia*, a great book which spread his fame quickly. With him he carried letters of invitation from the Archbishop of Canterbury and his old pupil Mountjoy; and before he had been long in England, these bore their promised fruit, a living from the one, a pension from the other. The King and Wolsey, Fox and Ruthall, soon showed favour; Fisher, as Chancellor of Cambridge, sent him down to hold the Lady Margaret's chair. There at length came leisure to work in the field to which Colet had bidden him. He took up the New Testament again; Jerome again, at whom he had worked in Paris in 1500; and Seneca, who was always to him a seeker after God, to be loved almost like a Christian. For two or three years in the quiet quadrangles of Queens'—desolate sometimes because of the plague—he went on steadily with his preparations. Then, by a mischance, which was possibly an artifice of his own, he was brought into touch with Froben, the prince of printers, and began upon his immense career of output. From that time forward there was no wavering: the rest of his life was to be given to sacred learning.

In resuming the New Testament after the translation he had made in 1505-6, his first idea was to produce a volume of notes. At Cambridge he certainly worked upon the Greek text, having plenty of manuscripts at his command. When he reached Basle in August 1514 there was discussion of the form of the book and what it should include. It is often stated that Froben and Erasmus put their heads together and formed the plan of hurrying out an edition of the New Testament in Greek, to anticipate Ximenes' great Bible which was pursuing its leisurely way through the press at Alcalá. I cannot find that this is more than an ingenious conjecture. It may have been well known at Basle that Ximenes' scholars were at work; for manuscripts had been lent to Alcalá from Venice and Rome, and the New Testament had in fact been completed by January 1514, though it was not yet published. But there is no evidence for this alleged competition. The negotiations between Erasmus and Froben show no sign of haste until more than a year later. In September 1514 a proposal was made for a Greek text with Erasmus' translation and notes; but then he appears to have drawn back. In the spring he was hesitating whether the book would not be better printed in Italy; and when he returned to England in April to fetch his translation and to look again at manuscripts of Jerome, he was followed by urgent letters in which Froben begged to be allowed to have the New Testament at any price.

Erasmus was back in Basle by July 1515, and then at length an agreement was reached; but it was not till the latter part of September that the book really began to advance, when two competent young men were installed to see it through the press, Nicholas Gerbell and Oecolampadius, afterwards the famous Reformer. Then the printing-house exerted all its resources, and within six months a book of nearly one thousand pages, with Greek and Latin type mingling continually, was published to the world. If there had been any intention of competing with Ximenes, the design would naturally have been concealed. But in fact Erasmus wrote openly from the first about his project, and one of the letters was in print by December 1514 in his *De Copia*, an educational work designed for wide circulation. Nor are there any paeans of victory after success. It seems more likely that the idea of a Greek New Testament was in the air, as a result of the invention of printing; and that at Alcalá and Basle men were working simultaneously without knowledge of each other.

The manner of the preparation of the text illustrates the standard of the age in critical scholarship. Erasmus had expected to find good Greek manuscripts at Basle— apparently he could not borrow one in England to take out with him, or perhaps he did not wish to carry so weighty a package. On arriving he obtained from the Amorbachs the loan of five; but, to his disappointment, none was good enough to send straight to the printers. He was obliged to go through one, of the fifteenth century, and prepare it himself; and he gave to Gerbell and Oecolampadius a twelfth-century manuscript which had been used by Reuchlin, to help them in their correction. Then, as he found that they were using their own judgement more than he wished, he took this away and let them have one of the thirteenth century, which he considered more accurate; and they also had two other fifteenth-century manuscripts to refer to. Even so he was not satisfied; and in the end he had to undertake the final revision of each sheet of proof himself— a process which he considered should not have been necessary if the correctors had been equal to their work. For Revelation he borrowed another manuscript from Reuchlin; and, as the last few verses of the book were missing, he calmly translated them back from the Latin. Erasmus' text became later the basis of Robert Stephanus' of 1550, which is the received text of the Greek Bible in England; and therewith these few Greek verses for which there is no manuscript authority at all.

After the publication Erasmus was in no way content. He immediately began to prepare for a new edition, and took every opportunity to examine new manuscripts. The Regent Margaret lent him the Codex Aureus from the Royal Library at Malines; others came from St. Bavo's Abbey at Ghent, from Mount St. Agnes near Zwolle, from the priory of Corsendonk near Turnhout. Through Bombasius he consulted the Vatican manuscript now known as B. The Franciscans at Antwerp also lent him a manuscript. When at Bruges he examined some at St. Donatian's; at Constance those of the

Cathedral. Whether he collated all these completely or
merely examined the readings at doubtful points, he
never states. It was his custom to make his servant-
pupils read aloud to him in the afternoons when he
wished for relaxation; and in that way—then the regu-
lar method of collation—it would not have been difficult
to cover the ground rapidly, especially as some of the
manuscripts were only of parts of the New Testament.
Four times he edited the volume anew, in 1519, 1522,
1527, 1535, the Notes being amplified on each occasion.

The second part of his scheme was to open up the
Fathers, 'whom', as William Latimer wrote to him,
'few modern theologians read and none understand'.
The famous Basle printer, John Amorbach, had planned
standard texts of the four Doctors of the Church; Ambrose appeared in 1492, Augustine in 1506, and Jerome
succeeded. By 1508 the work was in hand, so that when
Erasmus returned from Italy, travelling from Constance
to Strasburg, no doubt through Basle, and so down the
Rhine, he probably learnt of the undertaking. As quite
a young man he had been interested in Jerome; and
when he left Oxford in 1499 to return to the wider opportunities of Paris, while learning Greek, he began working
at the Letters, attributing some of the depravation of
the text to a want of Greek in copyists of manuscripts.
At Cambridge, in 1511, he lectured on the Letters, and
busied himself again with the duties of an editor, as soon
as he had finished with the New Testament. Several
ancient manuscripts were before him, and they certainly
formed an important part of his foundations. In May
1512 he refused an offer from Badius to undertake an
edition of the Letters, which appears to have been discussed between them earlier; his reason very likely being
that he wished to take part in the Basle edition. For

that Reuchlin had helped with the Hebrew, and John Kuno, the Dominican, and Gregory Reisch, prior of the Carthusians at Freiburg, had done preparatory work on the Letters, which were to occupy four volumes out of the nine.

When Erasmus reached Basle in August 1514, he quickly took his place on the editorial staff, before any decision had been made about the New Testament. Reisch handsomely gave way to him, and by September he had settled down to his daily 'grind in the mill', often exclaiming that it cost him more effort to edit than it had cost Jerome to write. In the spring of 1515 he went to England, and took some of his 'copy' for revision with the manuscript; and on his return Jerome and the New Testament were in the press, side by side, controlled by his masterful hand. For six months the New Testament took precedence; as soon as it was finished, Jerome is in the last stages. We hear of a new manuscript borrowed from Reichenau in November 1515; in the summer of next year Beatus Rhenanus and Erasmus were writing prefaces in the names of the young Amorbachs, who were loyally carrying on their father's great undertaking. In September seven copies of the splendid edition—sixty-three great folio volumes—were sent after Erasmus to the Netherlands, part of the pay for his share in the undertaking; and thence he distributed them to his English friends, Warham, Colet, Fisher, Urswick, and More. Twice again during Erasmus' lifetime did the cry go up of his toil over Jerome. The nine volumes were printed by Froben in 1524–6, and by Chevallon at Paris in 1533; a new Froben issue appeared in 1536–7, just after his death, and of course not without his 'indefatigable diligence'.

After completing a thorough revision of the New

Testament early in 1519, Erasmus turned to Cyprian, whom on re-reading he considered to be almost equal in importance to Jerome. For the basis of his text he had three printed editions, ranging from 1471 to 1512, and two manuscripts, one lent from St. Germain-des-Prés, near Paris, the other from Gembloux, with a letter which offered to lend him the whole library of the house. He on his side promised to return the manuscript carefully. The work was quickly done; for the Gembloux manuscript did not reach him till June 1519, and the edition, one folio volume, appeared in February 1520. Erasmus was soon dissatisfied with it, however; a new edition, 'freed from innumerable faults', appeared in November 1521, and there are later revised issues of 1525 and 1530.

Meanwhile Augustine was claiming some of his attention. Already, in 1517, Froben had been planning a new edition more correct than Amorbach's of 1506; and for some time in 1518, and again in 1520–1, Erasmus worked away at the text. But two revised editions of the New Testament were called for, and he judged Augustine to be beyond his powers, at any rate for the time. So he persuaded Vives to undertake the popular *City of God* for immediate publication by Froben; procuring for him manuscripts from Cologne and Bruges. The 'copy' all passed through the hands of Erasmus, who contributed a preface for the title-leaf; and in September 1522 the book was published—a solid folio of nearly 800 pages, which Froben had difficulty in selling, because the price had been raised by the great bulk of the notes.

Erasmus might form his own plans of work, but he was always open to consider what offered, especially anything new. Early in 1522 the only known manuscript of Arnobius' commentary on the Psalms was discovered in the Austin house of Franckental near Worms, and

was sent to him through the Dean of Spires. In spite
of the roughness of the style he was attracted by the
terse directness, and proceeded to edit it for Froben to
print in a small folio. Like the Augustine it appeared in
September, in time for the autumn fair at Frankfort.
The friend who had procured Arnobius also produced
a manuscript of Hilary in May 1522; and in February
1523 Erasmus had edited another folio volume, compar-
ing the manuscript with the Paris printed edition of 1511.

The following year saw the revised edition of Jerome,
and 1525 opened with the third edition of Cyprian. Then
he began to break ground upon a larger task. The theologians were thinking what must the eloquence of Chrysostom be in his original Greek. Erasmus had urged an
edition upon Asulanus at Venice—'the world is mad for
sacred texts', he wrote; but as nothing came of the
proposal he persuaded Froben to publish a few small
volumes of translations, some with the Greek added.
He bought Greek manuscripts from Italy; but the magnitude of the task was slowly revealed to him. Much of
what was ascribed to Chrysostom proved to be spurious.
Then his servant-pupils had not enough Greek, and he
had to do all the copying and collation himself. His
health, too, was troubling him: for months at a time he
suffered agonies with the stone. 'This little body of mine
might be equal to the labours of my studies for some
years yet, if it weren't so repeatedly battered by this
terrible weapon. A man who has once given himself
wholly to obeying the will of God can die a thousand
deaths.' As with Augustine, therefore, he reluctantly
abandoned the attempt, and in spite of Giberti's brilliant
attempt, the world had to wait nearly a century before
Sir Henry Savile's energy and wealth produced the first
Greek Chrysostom, at Eton, in eight volumes.

Erasmus' next work was upon Irenaeus, the pupil of
Polycarp at Smyrna, who had become Bishop of Lyons.
Opinion in the learned world was divided as to whether
he had written in Latin or in Greek; and the question
was not settled till forty years later, when some Greek
fragments were found embedded in the works of Epi-
phanius. Erasmus inclined to the side of Latin, and
produced in 1526 the first Latin text in a small folio.
As far back as 1522 John Faber had promised to provide
him with a manuscript from Rome; but the ground of
Erasmus' text must have been two very ancient manuscripts which he says were lent by monastic houses. For
not till May 1526—three months before the book appeared—was Faber's promised manuscript delivered: so
that Erasmus can have made little use of it. Of the three
that were thus at his disposal not one has been traced.

Foiled of the Greek Chrysostom, Erasmus could not
lose any opportunity of working upon that attractive
Father, whose prayer in this life was for 'knowledge of
Thy truth'. One of his manuscripts sent from Venice—
now in the Bodleian, where later it served Savile—contained some homilies which had never been translated.
This piece of work he proceeded to execute, adding to
it some of the translations of 1525, a long treatise translated by his friend Germanus Brixius, and some versions
of Athanasius from a manuscript which he had lately
acquired, but which has not been identified. The volume
was published by Froben in 1527 for the spring Frankfort fair.

After this came Ambrose, the last big undertaking
that Froben lived to complete. The only edition yet in
existence was Amorbach's of 1492; which no doubt
served Erasmus as a basis, with other prints of separate
parts of Ambrose. He speaks vaguely, too, of manu-

scripts which he had used: very ancient, but he gives nothing more definite about them. A commentary on Hebrews had been reported to him from England in 1520, and a friend had copied out a page for him to examine; but on grounds of style he quickly determined that the ascription to Ambrose was a mistake, and rejected it. In 1523 he displays some acquaintance with the text; in April 1526 he reports that nothing will be done about the edition that year, because Froben's partners were obstructive. Nevertheless the four folio volumes were completed within a year of Irenaeus: but this time Erasmus enlisted the help of the young Bohemian Sigismund Gelenius, without which so large an undertaking could hardly have been carried through in time for the autumn fair. The Benedictines of St. Maur, in editing Ambrose a century and a half later, considered that Erasmus had not made enough use of manuscripts, but had relied too much on the medieval method of conjecture.

As Ambrose passed out of the press, Augustine took its place. Froben was still hankering after his new edition. In the winter of 1524–5 Erasmus had been persuaded to begin work again. First he was cajoled into looking at a few pages; then he would undertake the Letters; finally he made himself responsible for the whole, hoping to get help from his Louvain friends, Martin Lypsius, Vives, and Dorp. But no help was ready, and again the scheme was dropped, till 1527, when, though reluctant, he shouldered the whole burden to please his incomparable friend. When Froben died in October 1527, two volumes were printed out of ten, and thenceforward Erasmus had everything upon him. 'It is killing me', he cries repeatedly in his letters: 'I have to keep seven presses going at a time.' 'Duty drives me: otherwise I wouldn't have taken all this trouble, not for

1,000 florins'—a sum which would have kept him in board and lodging for five years. Or again, 'I shall die of this; there are so many blunders, and the author is interminable. Others might have brought more learning to it, but no one would have taken such pains. There will be no notes such as I wrote for Jerome; all I do is to correct mistakes and arrange the material to show what is spurious.' 'In the time I have given to Augustine I could have finished off all my own plans of work.' Then, as the port looms nearer, hope revives: 'When this is done, I shall begin on something greater.'

He states that he had used manuscripts, but the only one that he mentions definitely was from Gembloux, a bad text which he had borrowed in his Louvain days. The matter of Augustine was difficult, the style involved and obscure, claiming the editor's constant attention: 'I have corrected hundreds of portentous blunders; the book will be quite different from what it was.' As he has so little to say of his sources, it seems likely that much of his work was done with printed texts, of which there were already many in existence, of separate parts, reading them through and emending them by conjecture.

With all this toil Augustine was achieved in 1529, ten stout folio volumes. Simultaneously the Froben firm printed a new edition of Erasmus' Seneca, revised with the help of other prints; and a small treatise by Lactantius, for which Erasmus had revised the Aldine text from a manuscript. The migration to Freiburg necessarily disturbed his plans of work, and all through the summer of 1530 his health was wretched. He did little more, therefore, than write prefaces for the printers. In 1530 the Frobens produced a Latin Chrysostom in five folio volumes, incorporating translations by Erasmus and earlier hands, also by Capito and Oecolampadius with whom he was now bitterly at variance: so that though he contributed a preface and a life of Chrysostom, the general supervision can hardly be ascribed to him. In the same year he gave the Freiburg printer, Faber Emmeus, a preface for a treatise on the Eucharist by the Cluny Benedictine Algerus (†1130); a work hitherto unknown. The manuscript had been recovered, with another unknown treatise by Guimund, bishop of Aversa near Naples (*c.* 1080), from a well in the monastery of Marbach near Colmar: into which it had been cast during the frenzies of the Peasants' Revolt. The same monastery provided him later with an unpublished commentary on the Psalms by Haymo, bishop of Halberstadt (†853); which Faber Emmeus published in 1533. Here again it seems likely that Erasmus was only responsible for the preface.

In 1531 his health for a time improved. In May he wrote a preface for some translations from Gregory Nazianzen made by his friend Pirckheimer, which the Frobens printed in September. And then he encouraged them to a Greek Basil, the first edition, collecting everything he could lay his hands on. He makes no mention of the manuscripts used; but it seems likely that he directed the whole enterprise.

Next he gave all his efforts to finishing a work on preaching, the *Ecclesiastes*, which he had had in hand for twelve years, and which his friends had long been urging him to publish. 'They tell me', he writes, 'that if I am to live, I must give up all writing, indeed study of any sort. But life at such a price is no life, especially as my pains will not give me up.' The *Ecclesiastes* was completed in 1535, and he went back to Basle to see it through the press, a small folio of 450 pages. He even thought of fulfilling his oft-made promise of returning

to the Netherlands; but his gout grew worse, and he was
confined to his room in Jerome Froben's airy house, Zum
Luft. From the autumn onwards he left it only once,
and most of his time was spent in bed. In spite of all, he
could not rest from labour, and began upon a Latin
edition of Origen, a Father in whom he had been interested for his bold critical spirit ever since 1501.
Whenever his pains remitted, he went on; but he was
not destined to finish. The two folio volumes of the
Froben edition did not appear till three months after
his death.

Such in outline was Erasmus' work for the serious
study of divinity. Side by side with it went on a series
of other publications, small and great in many fields,
which might have seemed a life's output for any private
man. In his last twenty years came seven new issues of
the *Adagia* revised and enlarged; editions of Curtius,
Suetonius, Pliny's *Natural History*, Livy, Terence; Aristotle and Demosthenes in the Greek; with small volumes
of separate treatises by Cicero, translations from Plutarch and Galen and Xenophon; commentaries on ten
of the Psalms, and other devotional books; a book on
Letter writing; moral essays on the Tongue, and on
Christian marriage and widowhood; controversies with
keen adversaries, and a direct attack on Luther; the
Colloquies continually expanding in ten editions; his
Paraphrases of the whole New Testament except the last
book. His work as editor of the classics did not always
amount to a great deal; but even so the bulk of this
secondary work remains great.

Erasmus' was not the temper of a scholar as we understand it to-day; yet he chose to give his life to scholarship, and gave it abundantly. Not for him was the slow
labour of digging foundations and laying brick to brick

to build up an edifice. His work was always done in heat, under the passion of his demand for knowledge. He read, he wrote, *tumultuarie, praecipitanter*. When he had formed a design, he liked to carry it out *vno impetu*. To those round him he was the leader, whose will was their driving force, sweeping them on to keep pace with him. His sense of what was business-like led them to the newest methods of sparing labour, his view that economy may be of time rather than money prompted them to avoid petty savings. It is an interesting point, though it may be nothing more than a coincidence, that before he came to Venice, most of Aldus' books had no numbers to their pages: from the date of his visit books with unnumbered pages almost disappear. The Neacademia marvelled at this Northerner who could do the work of two; and though later, in revenge for his acid sketch of Asulanus' niggard housekeeping, they depicted him as grossly guttling and guzzling among them, there was never any doubt as to the amount that he achieved. With Budaeus and with his cherished friend Beatus Rhenanus he understood the importance of using manuscripts; but palaeography was as yet hardly born, and like Bentley, two centuries later, he relied more upon his own gift of swift divination.

In his ways, too, he was magnificent. As soon as he could afford it, even before he could afford it, he must have a horse to ride and a servant to attend on him, books to work upon, leisure and quiet. His use of paper reveals him. However costly the wars might make it, there is no sparing. His margins are ample, his lines well spaced and handsomely framed upon the page. So, too, in using his books, the Aldine Aristotle which is at Wells, the Aldine Athenaeus in the Bodleian, he writes with his rapid hand in the margin any word that catches his interest: once a French proverb with which he translates the Greek.

The world into which he was born was still mainly medieval: then, as he grew to manhood, he saw a new invention offering enlarged possibilities of knowledge. Looking about him he beheld others gathering, gathering always, and never securing their treasure trove: Grocin collecting Greek manuscripts and reading diligently all his life long, or that shy scholar William Latimer, sipping the sweetness of one subject after another, yet neither of them committing their learning to the exposure of the printed page with all its hazard of error. To teach orally, to quicken interest, to inspire—all these were good. But they were not enough. His own action he resolved should be different. First to prepare, and then to print, as much as ever he could: that was how he would do God service.

The serious character of his life-work has been misunderstood, partly through the variety of his genius, and partly because of the words in which he describes over and over again the aim of his great quest—words which to modern ears are misleading. *Linguae et bonae literae, politior literatura* have a dilettante sound to us, as though elegance and grace and finished beauty of style were the end, with the ornament given by command of many tongues. Erasmus writes with conviction: 'Without languages and polite learning all branches of study are numb, speechless, almost blind; states languish, and life loses its value; man is hardly man at all.' The languages he sought were those three which to Jerome enshrined the Bible, which Augustine would master in order to understand Scripture; the good learning was that which to us accompanies godliness. Languages alone without learning did not exhaust the requirements of education;

and the learning must be decisively Christian, not, as in
Italy, tinged with paganism.

This was the basis of his fame in his own day. To all
but the incurably conservative he was the leader, the
man of untiring energy, who was bringing new life to
sacred study, making it real and concrete, founded upon
ascertained fact. From many a monastic house, men he
had never heard of wrote to court his acquaintance and
profit by his learning, Luther among the number. In
1524 to Giberti the datary, promoter of that splendid
fragment of a Greek Chrysostom, he was the man who
had brought polite learning into Germany, with the piety
and elegance of his writings. From Spain a Vicar-general
wrote to him in 1526 that men and women of every class
admired and almost worshipped his stupendous erudition, aspiring to fight under the banner of this champion
of the sound study of Christian antiquity. His opponents
among the monks and friars, being forbidden to speak
against him publicly, had been defaming him in private,
especially among the women; with the result that there
was a wide demand for his writings, which were being
translated into Spanish. Even the nuns behind their
bars were clamouring for his books; and if these were
denied by authority, were getting them secretly introduced into the recesses of their convents. From England in 1528 Polydore Vergil wrote, 'Every one is saying that your unrivalled learning has made you immortal
already.'

Erasmus is often contrasted with Luther, as though
the gulf between them had been as impassable as their
language—shouts of anger in the midst of struggle—
was uncompromising. The difference was, however, not
of aims but of method. Each sought first the kingdom
of God and His righteousness, but for climbing thither

each had another way. Luther could buy a Homer, and lament that he had no time to read the classics; but his heart was set, in his chamber and in his pulpit, on cultivating a sense of sin. In the presence of his Maker that was his dominant thought. Erasmus found high value in simple goodness; all his life he set it forth and showed it accordingly. But *his* prayer was for a sense of ignorance. Reason to him was God's best gift to man, and for reason to have her perfect work, man must gather knowledge. Upon this quest he was ever in the van, drawing men to follow by his persuasive charm, shaming them into participation by his unsparing faithfulness. Long life was given to him, which he filled with toil; and at the end, when the band of loyal friends saw their master taken away from their head on that July day, they were left with a vision of his

> gray spirit yearning in desire
> To follow knowledge like a sinking star
> Beyond the utmost bound of human thought.

THE WRITINGS OF ERASMUS

INTO the career of Erasmus I do not propose to enter. There is abundant material, and his life has often been written. Seebohm has composed a careful and illuminating monograph on his relations with Colet and More. Jebb's Rede lecture is clear and suggestive. Mr. F. M. Nichols has woven a narrative of his life round Translations of the Letters. But for a vivid and penetrating sketch of Erasmus' attractive personality you cannot do better than turn to the pages of Froude. There was much in common between the biographer and his subject; in charm of character, in variety of experience, in brilliance of gifts. And though it is true that Froude's book has many blunders in points of fact and detail— blunders which a competent secretary might have served to avert—it is also true that no Life of Erasmus can approach Froude's for sympathy and insight and understanding. The outlines are boldly and truly drawn, as so remarkable a figure merits; and the reader feels throughout that he is reading of a real man.

I propose, therefore, to leave biography aside, except incidentally; and I shall try rather by examination of Erasmus' more important works to show the position that he held among his contemporaries; also to estimate his attitude towards and his services to literature. There are, however, a few points in his life to which I wish to draw your attention. Firstly, his years in the monastery at Steyn; where, despite the impression that he often gives, he managed to study widely and make himself acquainted with the classics and the Fathers. Secondly, the gradual change in the character of his work. In his earlier Paris period he was still a student; his only com-

positions of note being little treatises, the germs of his
educational books, written then for the use of his pupils,
and afterwards amplified almost beyond recognition,
when he had learnt more and no longer needed to teach.
In England his attention is turned to theology; and on
his second and third visits, under the encouragement of
Colet and Fisher, the preparation for his life's work was
done. Then, when he had established connexion with
Basle and its great printing resources, comes the splendid
series of editions of the Fathers. Finally, the variety of
his output must be noticed—he ventured into many
fields, and everywhere with success. As they came out,
his works were purchased by thousands, and aroused
applause or indignation, according to the side which the
reader took in the bitter controversies of the age. But
now those controversies are dead, or at least have as-
sumed other forms; studies have progressed, and have
passed on to new enquiries. Of all that Erasmus wrote
the modern world knows very little. Even the Paraphrases of the New Testament, which, as translated by
the Princess Mary and others, Injunctions of Edward VI
and Elizabeth required to be placed in every English
church, are now chiefly known to antiquarians. The
Praise of Folly and his Dialogues are read for their
intrinsic interest; but otherwise his works have ceased
to be anything more than a source for the history of
the period, though a source of the highest value and
importance.

In order to estimate the value of his achievement, we
cannot do better than examine in detail his two most
notable compositions, the *Adagia* and the New Testament; each of which passed through nearly a hundred
authorized and unauthorized editions.

The *Adagia* was composed in Paris, after Erasmus'

return from his first visit to England. The purpose of the book was to help those who wished to write elegant Latin by providing them with neat sayings and literary allusions to be scattered about their sentences. Moreover each adage was explained in a few words, and indications were given of different ways in which it could be used. A few specimens will show its character. 'Herculei labores (No. 13): proverbially used of undertakings which are useful to others, but to their authors bring nothing but reproach.' 'Cantharus aquilam querit (fo. 47 vᵒ): taken from the fable: the beetle, to avenge an insult, cast the eagle's eggs out of the nest. It may be used of people who wish to be revenged on one who has annoyed them by doing him an injury. The Greek is αἰετὸν κάνθαρος μαιεύεται.' 'Ignem gladio ne fodias: (fo. 10 vᵒ): that is, do not provoke an angry and proud man with abuse.' In June 1500 the little volume appeared in Paris, with the title *Veterum maximeque insignium paroemiarum, id est adagiorum, collectanea,* and containing 818 adages. But the Latin-writing public was numerous. The book sold well, and his friends advised him that he might well have made it larger and less jejune in its treatment. He was not slow to take advice, and keeping his eyes open began to prepare for something different. In 1505 he had the book issued again by his original printer; and in 1506, as he passed through Paris on his way to Italy, he gave it to Badius to print, with twenty more adages. The demand for the book in this small form was not exhausted: till 1543 it continued to find a public in France and Germany, and saw thirty-two more reprints; although to its author it had long been dead.

Erasmus went to Italy with some pupils, not to teach them but to advise about their studies. For a year he sat with them beside the leaning towers of Bologna, working for his own purposes, no doubt upon the *Adagia*. At the end of that time his engagement was finished, and he betook himself to Venice, where he had made friends with Aldus Manutius. The great printer's house was rightly called an Academy. He had gathered round him a band of learned scholars; from far and near manuscripts were sent to him with nothing more than the request that he should print them; and there was a rich store of books. Erasmus set to work, laying hands on Greek authors whom he had not found before, and the essence of all that he read found its way into the new *Adagia*, which Aldus had undertaken to print. The presses creaked, and the type rattled in the compositors' cases; and amongst them sat Erasmus at his great table, surrounded with books, and paper of the best, reading and collecting and noting, inserting a long passage here, there dashing out a whole page and rewriting with new thoughts and wise instances. As fast as he could write, the sheets were carried off to be set up; and in nine months Aldus issued to the world an almost new book, the *Adagiorum Chiliades*. It was indeed a contrast, between the little Paris quarto and the Aldine folio. The leaves had risen from 90 to 275, the adages from 838 to 3,260; and now the wealth of Greek literature was enriching the work, the Greek for which Erasmus in 1499 had declined all Colet's inducements to stay in Oxford, the Greek 'without knowledge of which we are nothing', as Colet—who had not learnt it—wrote to him later, in a sort of confession.

But the book had not yet reached its limit. When Fisher had established Erasmus at Queens' within reach of the libraries of Cambridge, and Warham had given him a pension from the living of Aldington, ease and opportunity induced him to give the *Chiliades* another birth. A hundred and fifty new adages were inserted, but this was not the only change; for the book became a quarter as large again as it had been before. This increase in bulk was due to the expansion of some of the notes on individual adages into complete essays, in which Erasmus expatiated on subjects that were near his heart, his friends and his work, stories that amused him, or the new ideas which, then as now, were in the air. The most famous of these are three: *Sileni Alcibiadis* (No. 2201), the *Scarabeus* (No. 2601), and *Bellum* (No. 3001), which were shortly afterwards reprinted separately, and have been translated into German, French, Dutch, Spanish, English, and Welsh. The first refers to Socrates, a Silenus hideous to behold but a temple of the virtues within; and the thought suggests its contrary, the men whom that age knew only too well, popes and bishops, kings and nobles, lapped in pomp and circumstance and holden with pride in the plenitude of their power, but inwardly contemptuous of their subjects and careless of God's poor. The *Scarabeus* draws him again to this theme. We have seen how briefly he handled the same text in 1500. *Scarabeus aquilam quaerit*—the beetle attacks the eagle. Now it suggests to him the inequality of the struggle between the king of the air and the poor creature that we tread upon, and calls up again the thought of the mighty monarch riding on imperturbable to his own ends, and only conscious of those to whom he should owe duties when in leisure moments he gives thanks to God 'who subdueth the people that is under me'. Finally in the *Bellum*, expanded from a few lines to sixteen folio pages, Erasmus pours forth his eloquence on a great argument, to which he returned again and again throughout his life—'Sweet is war to those who know it not'; but Erasmus, like all too many in that splendid age, knew it only too well. His words were winged, and soar still without coming to earth; indeed, an English translation of them was printed ten times during the nineteenth century by the Society of Friends, that unflinching body who pursue peace in the conviction that war cannot be reconciled with the religion they profess.

In two other adages, *Festina lente* (No. 1001) and *Herculei labores* (2001)—you will notice how he chooses the first numbers of hundreds or thousands at which to place these expatiations; perhaps to introduce divisions into a somewhat shapeless mass—he describes his labours over this great book. They only ended with his life; for seven times more he brought it to new birth. The last edition, which reached 580 folios with 4,151 adages, appeared within a few months of his death.

The following excerpt from the adage *Festina lente* will show something of the book in its new form:

'This is not the place to dwell on the many ways in which our great men waste their money; in gaming, drinking and debauchery, in unnecessary journeys, in processions and petty wars, in retinues of idle servants. If only they would spare a fraction of their squanderings to help on good undertakings! Aldus in his great tasks has the support and encouragement of men of learning, who seek to lighten his labours. From as far off as Hungary and Poland ancient manuscripts are sent to him for publication; unsought, and indeed with presents of money. What Aldus did in Italy—for now, alas, he is dead, though his name still lends credit to the firm—Froben is doing on this side of the Alps with equal determination and no little skill, but not with equal recompense; for in our country literary enterprise does not find such support as it does in Italy. See how magnanimously the Italians treated a Dutchman. When I was there editing the *Adagia*, all the scholars of their own accord lent me unprinted manuscripts which they thought might be useful to me; Aldus, John Lascaris, Egnatius, Musurus, and Frater Urbanus, besides many others whom I knew neither by name nor by sight. I had brought nothing with me to Venice except a disordered mass of material. It was great rashness, but I let Aldus begin printing at once. In about nine months the whole book was finished, although I had been ill with stone, my first experience of that trial. How much the work would have lost, without the manuscripts which were lent to me! Plato, Plutarch, Athenaeus, Pausanias, Pindar, the proverbs of Apostolius supplied by Aleander, and innumerable others. Compare with this the conduct of a certain northern friend of mine; he is still one, for we must take our friends as they are, not quarrel with them. When I was preparing for the Venice edition, I happened to observe that he had a Suidas with some proverbs noted in the margin. It was a big book with a lot of pages to turn over, so I asked for the loan of it for a few hours, for my boy to transcribe the notes into my copy. Nothing of the sort. After repeated entreaties I enquired whether he was going to publish a book of proverbs himself; if so, I would gladly give way to him. No, that was not it. At last I got it out of him: he considered them some of the secrets by which the learned retain the admiration of the populace, and so did not wish them published abroad. That was all! There are colleges and monasteries in Germany and France and England where very old manuscripts are treasured up; so carefully that either their very existence is denied, or if you are allowed to see them, you have to pay ten times what would be their price if printed. In the end, after all this care, they will just decay; unless thieves carry them off first.

'The nobles of those countries will not help learning. Money spent on it they regard as lost; and they dislike any undertaking which does not bring in a direct return. If only they were as generous as the Italians, Froben's dove and serpents would soon be as famous as Aldus' dolphins.'

The second work that we are to take as typical of Erasmus' life-work is the New Testament. On his first visit to England in 1499, when he was sent by his patron to spend a few months at St. Mary's College in Oxford, he came under the influence of Colet of Magdalen. The two young men, showing a common enthusiasm for learning and for righteousness, formed a friendship which lasted firmly for the twenty years remaining of Colet's life. Colet was lecturing on the Epistle to the Romans with great success, and he urged his foreign visitor to stay and fire the chilly studies of Oxford by expounding some part of the Old Testament—Moses or Isaiah. But Erasmus knew that for such a task he was inadequately equipped. He had no Greek, or Hebrew; so, penniless though he was, he went back to France to learn these languages. After four years, he reported himself again to Colet, to the rich young man—son of a Lord Mayor of London—who had now become D.D. and Dean of St. Paul's. In patrons' houses he had written a commentary on Romans, Colet's own subject—four volumes of it, a work which has never seen the light. In an abbey near Louvain he had found a work which was to set the standard for him in his future studies, and brought it back to Paris to be printed—Annotations on the New Testament by Lorenzo Valla, the audacious Canon of the Lateran, who had cast doubts on the Donation of Constantine, and with whose critical temperament Erasmus was much in sympathy. He had learned Greek, he said, and picked up a little Hebrew; and now he was panting to get to work. Could the Dean help him?

Colet's answer can be imagined. In a few months Erasmus was back in England. Most of his time was spent in London; and when he started for Italy in June 1506, he left behind in the hands of Colet's amanuensis a new translation of the New Testament, made from Greek manuscripts of which nothing is known.[1] Colet

[1] The early date of this translation, a fact discovered by the late

had lent him two Latin manuscripts from the Cathedral Library, but of the Greek manuscripts used there is no trace. While Erasmus was in Italy, Colet's one-eyed scribe, Peter Meghen of Hertogenbosch, leisurely copied out the translation on a magnificent scale, taking three years over the task. The splendid manuscripts in three volumes (of which one is now at Cambridge, the other two in the British Museum) were a present to the Lord Mayor from his son. In the Corpus (Oxford) Library is another copy, by the same hand, smaller but executed with great beauty: when or for whom it was made, there is no evidence—possibly it may have been given to Fox, the Founder of Corpus, who thought very highly of Erasmus, or it may be a special copy written for presentation to Henry VIII.

Why Erasmus began with a new translation there is nothing to show: possibly Valla's criticisms had pointed out many corrections that needed making in the Vulgate. His next step was to examine the Greek text. This he did while at Cambridge in 1512–13, employing four Greek manuscripts, one of which has been identified as written in England by a Byzantine scribe in the fifteenth century. In the summer of 1514 he set out for Basle, to make acquaintance with the printer Froben, and to arrange for publication. His first idea seems to have been to produce a volume of Annotations like Valla's. To print a Greek text would require more type than any printer north of the Alps then had, except

Bishop John Wordsworth, is not without interest. Foxe, in the *Book of Martyrs*, related as an instance of Thomas Cromwell's wonderful memory, that on his way to Rome in 1510 he learned by heart large portions of Erasmus' Translation of the New Testament. Mr. Gairdner, in the *Dictionary of National Biography*, rejects the story on the ground that the translation had not yet appeared. It would seem that here, as elsewhere, Foxe may be more trustworthy than is sometimes supposed.

possibly Froben. For some months Erasmus was not sure whether he would stay in Basle or go on to Italy; the question of type being perhaps the cause of his delay. Proposals were made, however, for an edition in the Greek with Erasmus' translation side by side and his notes at the end. But it was not until a year after his arrival that the work was definitely taken in hand. In August 1515 a beginning was made with the printing; and by February 1516 it was complete. Thus Colet's encouragement had led after sixteen years to the first printed text of the Greek Testament being given to the world. Two years earlier another edition had been printed—part of Ximenes' great Polyglott Bible. But awaiting the completion of the Old Testament in Hebrew and Greek and Latin, it was lying hid in the printing-house at Alcalá, not to appear in public till Leo X in 1520 gave permission.

Erasmus' volume was dedicated to the Pope; and in the second edition, 1519, appeared a Papal brief of September 1518 highly commending the work. Besides securing this demonstration of favour in high places, Erasmus protected himself against criticism by various introductory essays. There is an exhortation to all Christians to read the Bible; in which occurs the eloquent passage often quoted. Then an *Apologia* in which he explains his method, showing how by collation of manuscripts a text may be improved; and claiming the right to submit the Gospels to this process, like all other books. After this he reviews a few solecisms made by the Translator, evident and inexcusable; then passages obscure, passages evidently corrupt, passages added or cut out.

The New Testament went through five editions (1516, 1519, 1522, 1527, 1535), in each the notes amplified, till they form a large volume by themselves. Having completed his New Testament, Erasmus began to think of further work in the same field. He had set up a text with such material as he had at hand—except the Codex Vaticanus (B), none of the great manuscripts had then washed up on the beach of Time; he had made a new translation; and he had written notes which he was prepared to amplify indefinitely. But his high purpose went further. Having encouraged men to read the Bible, it now seemed a good thing to offer them a commentary. In 1501 he had written with his facile pen four volumes about the Epistle to the Romans, and now he took it up again. When it was printed, he styled it a Paraphrase; but by this he explained that he meant a kind of commentary, in which he felt at liberty to expatiate on subjects which the text suggested to him, free from the restrictions imposed by a literal translation or by a scholarly commentary. The book was printed in November 1517, with a dedication to Grimani, one of the leading Cardinals at Rome.

During the next four years he progressed steadily through the Epistles; and then at the request of another Cardinal he began upon the Gospels, in the order Matthew, John, Luke, and Mark, dedicated to the four puissant princes of Christendom, Charles and Ferdinand, Henry and Francis. In 1524 followed the Acts: Revelation he felt himself unequal to handling.

The success of the Paraphrases was immense. Edition after edition came out, authorized or pirated—for the idea of copyright had little power. By 1530 they had been wholly translated into German; in 1542 St. Matthew was available to the Bohemians, a people who had much sympathy with Erasmus; in 1543 there was a complete translation into French.

For us there is special interest in the treatment of the Paraphrases in England. In 1534 a wandering scholar, Leonard Cox of Thame in Oxfordshire, who had taught school in Hungary and Poland, translated Titus for dedication to Thomas Cromwell, a rare little volume of which only two copies are known to exist. But in 1543 Queen Katherine Parr, that courageous lady who dared to be 'No. 6', conferring with her neighbour the Head Master of Eton, Nicholas Udall, projected a complete translation of the Paraphrases. A number of scholars were set to work, Miles Coverdale, Thomas Key, Fellow of All Souls, Edmund Allen of Corpus (Cambridge), Francis Mallet, another Cambridge man who was to help the Princess Mary (about thirty) in translating the Gospel of St. John. The first volume was finished in 1548; the whole by 1549. A second edition appeared in 1552. In preparation for its appearance Injunctions were issued in the name of Edward VI, 1547. These were renewed in 1559, with some variations.

It has been questioned how far the Injunctions were obeyed; and it is said that few copies can be actually traced in contemporary records. It is a matter worth looking into, if sufficient material can be gathered. But at least it is certain that the book was diffused throughout England, and probably read.

Two small points are worth mentioning. In the copy of the Metsys portrait at Hampton Court Erasmus is depicted as writing the first words of the Paraphrase on Romans. In the Holbein portrait at the Louvre he is writing the opening words of his Paraphrase on St. Mark. The other point is that no College Library in Oxford possesses a copy of the Paraphrases in English—the University, when the book appeared, had no Library of its own.

These are two sides of Erasmus' work. He brought out the New Testament in Greek, the first edition to appear; and under the title of Paraphrases he produced a commentary of interpretation, which had a world-wide success. 'Of whom the world was not worthy.' His faith in light and knowledge, his loyal devotion of all his powers to the furtherance of this great cause, brought him enthusiastic friends and admirers. 'Most of what I know of Christ I have learned from Erasmus', wrote the Bishop of Augsburg in 1537. 'Erasmus has taught me to find in Christ the Way, the Truth and the Life, and to trust in Him alone', wrote a Carthusian from Flanders in 1528. 'There was nothing in his life which was not worthy of Christ', wrote a man who had been his confessor. But besides all this, his work brought him great obloquy. Jerome in his day had suffered persecution for daring to improve on the Old Latin Versions of the Bible—the man now canonized as a saint was a heretic to the orthodox of his own age. So too with Erasmus. His translation and his notes were attacked, sometimes on the ground of scholarship, more often because they imperilled received interpretations of doctrine. In the first verse of St. John's Gospel he had dared to write *sermo* for *verbum*; and he had questioned the authorship of the Epistle to the Hebrews. Like a pack of dogs his critics fastened upon him in a dozen places at once, cheering themselves on with an utterance which Rumour, lying as usual, attributed to the Archbishop of Toledo: 'If Erasmus is a heretic, he ought to be burned.' 'They hate me worse than they hate Luther', he complained. Well they might. Luther had brought schism and was rending the Church asunder: his bludgeon-strokes did great mischief. But their hurt and damage was clear and evident; the Church had triumphed over schism in the past and would do so again. But Erasmus made the orthodox uneasy. It was not merely that they had to match themselves with the sharpest tongue in Europe, who could overwhelm them with ridicule. His brilliant retorts, swift and clean as rapier-thrusts, left them gasping, with no power of reply; uncomfortable, they could not tell what he was at. They saw in him a man who, while claiming in all sincerity perfect loyalty to the Church, was raising new and difficult questions to which there was no evident answer.

'Back to the Bible' was the cry of Luther and the various new leaders who kept pushing on his work further than he wished. When Zwingli brought the Reformation into Zurich, he argued for a whole morning in the Town Hall before the Great Council, basing all his statements on the three Bibles he had before him, Hebrew, and Greek, and Latin, and silencing all opposition from them. The question which Erasmus raised was 'What is the Bible?' Neither he nor his opponents saw where he was tending; if he could have foreseen, he would have been shocked, no doubt, but not deterred. For God to him was *Via, vita, veritas*; and Truth shirks no questions, however startling.

It was not surprising that the question should be raised. The Invention of printing had brought new standards of critical accuracy to the world of learning, and men were beginning to enquire as to the sources of their knowledge of the past. That, if you wish to know the meaning of a book, it is better to read it in the original than in a translation, seems to us a commonplace. In Colet's day it was just being learnt. In the 1490's Aldus' firm at Venice gave the philosophers Aristotle in the Greek; and then proposed a Bible in its original language for the theologians. The project failed, but was renewed a few years later in Spain, where Cardinal Ximenes

committed the great charge to his new university at Alcalá, and lived to see it carried through. Erasmus' work
stands in with these. It was no flash of originality: it
was just an attempt to furnish his generation with what
it was seeking, a text of the New Testament in Greek, to
be the foundation of more careful and more minute study.
As an achievement of scholarship it has long been super-
seded; but it remains the foundation of the learning of
to-day. Building upon it, starting from that point, men
have studied the tradition of the Bible on the same lines
as they have studied the tradition of all other literature.
And the Bible stands to-day, a book of supreme spiritual
value, written with human hands, handed down to us by
human means, and showing in its fortunes of survival
no trace of divine guidance or protection.

All Erasmus' writings, including his Letters, are in
Latin. Throughout most of his life he wrote and spoke
and thought in Latin. Almost unconsciously he had
made himself a master of Latin style. His Latin, like so
much else in his life, is a compromise. The schoolmen
had made the language flexible and apt to express all
shades of meaning: but in doing so had sacrificed every
consideration of elegance. Some of the scholars of the
Renaissance prided themselves on using no word that
was not in Cicero; and giving infinite thought to arrangement and poise and balance, they attained elegance at
the cost of stiffness and obscurity. Erasmus stands
between the two, thinking always of lucidity and com-
bining it with flexibility and grace. His words delight
the reader, yet his meaning is rarely doubtful, unless he
wishes it to be so.

The power of self-expression in this high degree is not
given to many. Those that possess it attach men easily
to themselves and hold them, if they be so minded, with

bonds that cannot be loosed: they also make many enemies. Erasmus had the power to sting as well as to stir,
and kept back none of his rich vocabulary when describing those with whom he differed; yet he was singularly
unconscious of the effect that his words had upon others.
'I cannot understand', he wrote to a friend, 'why some
people hate me so: I have never written a line to cast
a shadow of blackness upon the fame of any one.' 'Erasmus is a hollow nut', said Luther, after thinking of one
of those mordant sallies; 'Erasmus is a hollow nut, and
fouls the mouth.'

Very little that Erasmus wrote can be classed as pure
literature. There are a few unimportant poems; but,
apart from these, there is a very definite purpose, moral,
social, or political, running through all that he wrote;
and to this the considerations of art are always subordi-
nated. In the 'Praise of Folly' his wit and humour have
the fullest play, and the lightness and delicacy of his
touch is unequalled: yet all through, his eye is set steadily
upon the ills of the world that he wished to see amended.
Other seriously-minded Germans of that age had seen
its ills and sought to amend them. Brant in his *Ship
of Fools* pictured many kinds of them, each with a separate mark of folly; but his menacing blows scarcely
reached their aim. The broad buffoonery of the *Letters
of the Obscure Men* thumped like cudgels on the armour
of the foe; but there was more noise than damage. Erasmus' intention is just as serious, but he is an artist in
spite of himself. His Folly rose up to play, smiling,
dancing Folly, singing her own praise. Harmless, almost
charming, she seems as she comes on, with no sign of
danger; then in a trice her rapier has found out the joints
of the harness. The smarting victim stamped with

indignation. 'Folly', wrote a professor from Louvain, 'like Davus in the play is upsetting everything.' Years afterwards, when the field of battle had broadened and there were many assailants, it was to Folly's insidious attack that the sufferers traced the beginning of their misfortunes.

The form of literature in which Erasmus particularly delighted was the dialogue. His Colloquies, like so much else of his work, were of gradual growth. The first form of the book was drafted in his hungry days at Paris, and sold to a private coach; just a few forms of address, for the use of pupils, to teach them how to say in polite Latin, 'Pleased to meet you', 'So sorry to hear of your cold', or 'Good-bye, I must go'. After these came some brief conversations, without beginning or end, a few remarks interchanged, and nothing said. The composition did not merit the title of 'book', and Erasmus never thought of publishing it. But twenty years later Froben bought the manuscript from a rather questionable source and, without consulting the author, printed it at once. In self-defence Erasmus was obliged to put out a more correct edition at Louvain, where he was then residing. The book, slight though it was, proved successful from the first; edition after edition was sold, and any ill feeling between author and publisher was soon dispersed—indeed, a new edition in 1522 was dedicated by Erasmus to his godson, Froben's son, who was named after himself, Erasmus, later Erasmius, Froben. In that edition the first real Colloquy was introduced, a Banquet of religious men, which presents many typical characteristics of Erasmus' method; firstly, the vivid pictures of everyday life in the meeting of the guests, their general conversation before sitting down, dragging on till the host's wife sends to say that dinner will be spoiled unless they come; secondly, the serious topics and obvious morals; thirdly, the introduction of passages from Erasmus' own experience—the shrine of St. Thomas à Becket at Canterbury, the famous Carthusian monastery near Pavia, both of which induce the reflection that the wealth lavished on ornamenting these holy places had better have been given to the poor. The portraiture is life-like, and the conversation easy and bright, but there the artist ends. There is little attempt to draw character. It is in the matter that Erasmus is interested. His morals are plain and need no pointing; and he often goes off into diatribes against the follies and vices he saw around him.

In the next eleven years twelve new editions were produced, each, except one, amplified with new colloquies, varying from one to ten at a time: until the whole number reached forty-eight. The most brilliant of all, the *Iulius Exclusus*, Erasmus never dared to publish. It exhibited Julius II swaggering outside the gate of Heaven and amazed to find that Peter will not let him in.

It has sometimes been absurdly stated that Erasmus knew no modern languages. It is no doubt true that he had no proficiency in any one except his mother tongue, which he can hardly have forgotten entirely, even after years of speaking and writing Latin to such as could understand it. But the dialogue *De Pronunciatione* shows considerable familiarity with the phonetic value of the vowel-sounds in the principal languages and dialects of western Europe. And Beatus Rhenanus, who was beside his death-bed, records that his last words were in Dutch, 'Liever Got'. It is not to be supposed that a man who was continually travelling across Europe, often spending years at a time in the same country, should have acquired no knowledge at all of the languages he heard spoken around him. The following letter, however, written to two Cambridge friends, will show that he did not feel at ease in English. It concerns the father of one of his servant-pupils, who apparently was dissatisfied with Erasmus' treatment of his son:

'I cannot talk to this beast. You must make him understand that I have been more than a father to the boy; and that, so far from wasting his time, he has made more progress than he would have done in any school. I am detained here against my wishes, but I shall come on Wednesday with Watson. Goodbye, and treat this ass with some consideration, or he will be enraged with me. If Humphrey has time, I should like him to write out this letter ⟨to the father⟩ in English, and send it by John for me to sign.'

What interest Erasmus felt in modern languages is another question. The classical revival had inevitably thrust them for a time into the background, and few of the earlier humanists composed, as apart from translation, in anything but Latin; unless, like Brant and Reuchlin, they intended an appeal to the people. In the pages of Erasmus there are but few references to the nascent literature so soon to lift up its head and challenge the pre-eminence of the two great classical tongues. The name of Boccaccio is known to him only for his Latin writing. But there are two passages, which, separated by an interval of some years, indicate progressive sympathy towards the modern—as indeed was only to be expected: for Erasmus was too good a humanist to live only in the past. Both these passages deal with a subject for which the vernacular was necessary, *contiones ad populum*, preaching to the people. In writing a sketch of Colet's life in 1521 he describes how Colet had studied theology and law and history, and continues: 'England has men who have done for their country what Dante and Petrarch did for Italy': his allusion is probably to Gower and Chaucer; you will note that he does not call them poets. 'By studying their works Colet polished his diction, already preparing himself for preaching the Gospel.'

The second passage is in the *Ecclesiastes*, a treatise on preaching which had long been in his mind, but which he only completed in 1535. In the interval, fourteen years, the position had changed and he is more attentive to the moderns. He is speaking of the training of a preacher.

'The first requisite is to associate with people whose speech is pure and polished. The second is to listen to preachers of refinement. The third is to study the books of those who have attained to eloquence in the vulgar tongue: such as Dante and Petrarch among the Italians. Indeed there is no tongue so barbarous but that it has some elegance and expressiveness of its own, if it is properly developed. People who know Italian, Spanish and French well declare that in these languages, though debased derivatives, there is a charm which Latin never attains. The same is affirmed about English, though it is of mixed origin, and about German. In each of these men have written books worthy of high praise for eloquence. So the preacher to be need not fear to spend some portion of his time on books of this kind. The learned will think Latin and Greek more agreeable, but the true Christian will find no tongue barbarous by which he can win his neighbour for Christ. Only the affectation must be avoided of mixing in foreign words. How absurd it is for a preacher in Brabant to drag into his sermon French and Latin formations which will be lost on all who do not understand those tongues.'

Erasmus has many claims to fame. Of all that life brought him, I believe that he valued nothing more highly than that of which we have been able to make little mention here; the devoted attachment of his friends. His was an age of strife in which men's reputations were easily blackened. When one hears Erasmus belittled, it is well to remember that he was the chosen comrade of James Batt and Thomas More, the beloved master of Boniface Amerbach and Beatus Rhenanus.

ERASMUS ON CHURCH UNITY

'BEHOLD how good and joyful a thing it is, brethren, to dwell together in unity!' These words rise up frequently in men's thoughts to-day, when efforts are being made to promote one fellowship of all good Christian people: not without visions of a larger unity, of those who are on God's side, seeking him by divers paths, in following the light that has come into the world through divers prophets of God, yet surprisingly alike in the conceptions they form of the object of their quest.

At such a time it is interesting to consider another period when men's minds were much set upon unity, in the vain hope that they could extirpate diversity of opinion, otherwise called heresy, and therewith schism. I have made a translation of one of the compositions of Erasmus' later life, entitled *Liber de sarcienda Ecclesiae concordia*, 'About restoring concord in the Church', in the form of a commentary on Psalm 84: in which, after discoursing upon the actual words of the Psalmist, he concludes with some practical suggestions as to the restoration of unity, and indicates the spirit in which men should set about the task. It is usually more interesting to read a man's own words, even in a translation, rather than what other people say about him. Another point is that this treatise has never, so far as I know, been translated into English before: though translations of it into Flemish, German, and Danish were printed within a year of the book's first appearance in Latin—indeed the Netherlands, in their century of religious strife, saw many editions of both original and translation. What I am giving here is only a version of the latter part of the book, and is necessarily free. Erasmus' pen was as torrential as the most fluent orator's tongue, whirling along in eddies and backrushes which sometimes return almost to their starting-point: so that the sense is in places best set out by adaptation. I hope, however, that this exposition of his views is accurate.

But before we come to it, we must have a little about himself. He was born of uncertain parentage in 1466, and such as they were he had lost both parents by the time he reached fourteen. Left alone, except for a brother three years older, he drifted into a monastery, in pursuit of leisure for study—a hope in which he was not disappointed. Having exhausted the library of his priory, he got himself out of this immurement, and became a secretary to a bishop. Here too he found more restraint of his freedom than he desired; and the bishop let him go, to Paris University. For a few years he lived from hand to mouth, pursuing as best he could the studies on which he had set his heart—principally divinity. In 1499 an English pupil carried him off to this country; and in October he came up to Oxford, a freshman of thirty-three, except that he did not matriculate. Here he fell in with John Colet, a rich man's son, who had been to Italy and who without a fellowship had come back to Oxford to teach. The attraction between these two was instantaneous, each finding his counterpart in the other: the grave, serious-minded Englishman, his feet grounded upon the wealth of a Lord Mayor of London, and the brilliant, witty Dutch canon, with no resources but his amazing abilities and ready for any adventure. Their interests too were the same. Colet was lecturing on the New Testament, in a way that took Oxford by surprise: he urged his friend, who at the end of two months was preparing to take flight, to stay with him and lecture on the Old. Erasmus, more clear-sighted and not too old to surmount a new fence, replied that he must first go and learn Greek: 'without which', as Colet afterwards admitted, 'we are nothing'. He went and in five years came back, ready for his lifework. Colet, who had meanwhile become Dean of St. Paul's, supplied him with manuscripts from the Chapter Library, and led him on to attack the very centre of the position, to throw new light on the foundation of their religion, by a new translation of the New Testament.

From this time onwards, from 1506, Erasmus' career was settled. He was destined to be the leader of a new school of scientific study; bringing to bear upon sacred learning the critical scholarship which in the preceding century the Italians had applied almost exclusively to the classics. He was now forty, but his position was not yet assured. For three years he was in Italy, working with Aldus and visiting Rome: then for three years in Cambridge, working hard in Queens' College upon the New Testament and the text of Jerome. He courted the acquaintance of the great Basle printer, Froben, and left England in 1514 to work with him; and two years later there issued from Froben's press two books which mark an epoch in the study of divinity, the New Testament in Greek with a Latin translation and notes by Erasmus, and Jerome in nine folio volumes, for three of which, containing the letters, Erasmus was directly responsible.

He was now upon the pinnacle of his fame. On all sides the learned world acclaimed him as its leader without a rival, and hung admiringly upon his words. From various sources an income was assured to him, and he was free to devote the rest of his life to the advancement of theological study. The young Prince Charles, afterwards Charles V, made him one of his Councillors, and sent him to adorn the University of Louvain. There he began his famous series of Paraphrases upon the New Testament; but in 1521 he returned to Basle and to Froben, who printed for him in the next few years a whole gallery of the Fathers, about thirty folio volumes of them—Cyprian, Hilary, Jerome over again, Irenaeus, Ambrose, Augustine, Chrysostom in Latin, Gregory Nazianzen, Haymo, and finally Origen, upon which Erasmus was engaged at his death in 1536.

Such in brief was the course of his life. Throughout he showed himself a loyal member of the Church and a faithful servant of Christ. Besides his work in divinity he poured out a number of moral exhortations, encouraging men to simple straightforward goodness. His pen hit off the taste of the age, and what he wrote on these lines was widely read and translated into many tongues. Even when handling purely classical subjects, he would fly off occasionally into moral disquisitions, exposing the social and political evils of the time and showing what Christians could do to heal them. The same earnest purpose underlies his delicately witty satires, the Praise of Folly which its poor victims read as their own praise, or the first of his colloquies, the *Julius Exclusus*, which ridiculed the warlike Pope so audaciously that Erasmus never dared acknowledge it. The duty of a Christian man to make first himself, then other men, better was always in the forefront of his writings, and for this sake he reproved even kings.

What now was his position in the Church? He hated monastic life for himself and made haste to escape from it: not so much because he realized, as men were so soon to realize, that the institution on the scale which was then in use, was no longer necessary in more settled times, but because for his active and adventurous spirit freedom was the first requirement, freedom to act and move, freedom to read and think, freedom to deliver whatever message might be committed to him. Of abuses, wherever he saw them, he was an outspoken and unsparing critic; towards ignorance, especially when entrenched in high places, he was merciless. But by temperament he was entirely conservative. Fault he was always ready to find in details of the structure of Church and State; but the main fabric he regarded as good and natural growth under the ruling of God's providence, and on such an Ark the hand of man was not to be lightly laid. The freedom which he claimed for himself he would no more have allowed to the general company of all thoughtless people, than he would have placed a naked sword in the hands of a child.

To orthodox theologians, especially at the universities, he soon became suspect. To make a new translation of the New Testament was to reflect upon Jerome, the traditional author of the Vulgate; to promote the study of Greek was to draw dangerously close to a heretical church. Some of them too began to discover that the Praise of Folly was not so simple as it seemed. At Cambridge one college forbade that his New Testament should be brought within its walls; at Louvain bitter sermons were preached against him, and he was delated before the Rector, until, at the sacrifice of his Imperial pension, he sought quiet by returning to Froben at Basle.

Then came Luther, posting up on the church door at Wittenberg, like any other university student, the theses he was prepared to maintain for his degree. At first Erasmus gave him definite support, and wrote to prelates and princes to secure him a hearing. Then after the burning of the Bull and the condemnation at Worms he began to feel that Luther was going too far, and that schism was looming ahead. Luther on his side had no thought of schism. Like Wesley in a later age, he wished to reform the Church, but he had no idea either of leaving it or of being ejected. Before long, as the breach widened between Luther and the Church, Erasmus was entreated to take a side. He refused consistently, and became anathema to the extremists of both parties. It must not be forgotten, however, that with the moderates he was always in sympathy. Some of his best friends were monks and friars; with many of the less headstrong Reformers his relations were intimate.

By 1533, when he wrote the *Liber de sarcienda Ecclesiae concordia*, matters had gone far. The Peasants' Revolt of 1525 had shown what might come of disruption and chaos, if appeal were made to the masses. Luther had been left behind by his followers. Farel in the Jura, Oecolampadius in Basle, Zwingli in Zurich, were preaching new Gospels; and in 1531 the two latter had perished, Zwingli by the sword, in the armed conflict to which difference of religious opinions only too often leads. In 1529 a new form of worship had been set up at Basle, driving Erasmus for six of his last years to Freiburg. Images had been destroyed wholesale: at Zurich Platter, as sacristan of the Minster, finding that his stove would not burn, snatched St. John from one of the altars and thrust him into the fire, hoping that the congregation would not smell the paint. Scarcely a town of south Germany but had its body of Reformers, introducing new practices; many bishops and chapters withdrew into retirement. The inmates of monasteries and convents poured out into the world, marrying and returning to ordinary life. Even to Catholic Spain the infection spread. The Primate saw his province of Toledo swept by gusts of unintelligible religious ecstasy. Mobs of clergy and laymen, monks and nuns, young and old, clamoured for the Gospels, and down with the old law and the old ceremonies. Christian liberty was their demand, and fewer burdens for Christ's poor.

Under such conditions no wonder Erasmus felt that he must pray for the unity of the Church, and seek for something to save it from dissolving into atoms. His view might have been somewhat different if he could have foreseen the success with which the Lutheran Church in Germany, or later the English and Scottish Churches, organized themselves into self-governing and well-ordered communities. But as it was, the prime need seemed to be to preserve order, almost at any cost.

Before proceeding to our treatise there are two passages which may be considered, to illustrate the thought of that age upon the question of religious toleration. The first is from the *Utopia*. I need not dwell upon the close ties between Erasmus and More. Their hearts and minds were in complete sympathy, and when the *Utopia* appeared, men said that Erasmus must at any rate have written the first book. We may thus suppose that what More wrote was well known to Erasmus, and had very likely been discussed with him.

In the ninth chapter of the second book More describes the Utopian religion. There are many diverse kinds, he says, some worshipping for God the sun, some the moon, others one of the planets.

'There be that give worship to a man that was once of excellent virtue or of famous glory, not only as God, but also as the chiefest and highest God. But the most and the wisest part, rejecting all these, believe that there is a certain godly power unknown, everlasting, incomprehensible, inexplicable, far above the capacity and reach of man's wit, dispersed throughout all the world, not in bigness but in virtue and power. Him they call the Father of all. To him alone they attribute the beginnings, the increasings, the proceedings, the changes and the ends of all things.'

On hearing of the Christian religion, he goes on to say, many of them embraced it eagerly: until one of the converts began to wax so hot in its praise, that he did utterly despise all other, calling them profane, and the followers of them wicked and devilish, and the children of everlasting damnation. For such abuse of others he was sent into exile, 'for no law is more highly regarded among them than that no man's religion should be any hurt to him'.

Then he goes on to describe their public worship.

'The common sacrifices be so ordered that they be no derogation nor prejudice to any of the private sacrifices and religions. Therefore no image of any god is seen in the church; to the intent it may be free for every man to conceive God by their religion after what likeness and similitude they will. They call upon no name of God, but only Mithra; in the which word they all agree together in one nature of the divine majesty, whatsoever it be. No prayers be used but such as every man may boldly pronounce without the offending of any sect.'

Next let us glance at one of Erasmus' Colloquies, the *Inquisitio de fide*: which was no doubt written about the date of its publication, March 1524. This lends it significance. He was then just recovering from a very serious illness, and it seemed that life and strength could not hold out much longer. He made disposition of his possessions and wrote a short sketch of his life, the *Compendium vitae*, to serve as a basis for the fuller biography which he desired his friends to make. Under such circumstances the colloquy may well have been meant to put on record his religious opinions—a matter of evident concern to a man who for years past had been stigmatized as a heretic. One of the two speakers, Barbatius, has been so branded. His friend, Aulus, begins to question him, to find out what is amiss ; and ends by taking him through the Apostles' Creed, clause by clause. For some distance all goes well. The Descent into Hell is safely passed over in spite of the remarks of Cyprian and Tertullian. But at the question 'Do you believe in Holy Church?' Barbatius answers 'No'. This he proceeds to explain. 'I believe in a holy church, which is the body of Christ, that is a congregation of all men throughout the world who agree in the faith of the Gospel: to sever oneself from this is mortal crime. Cyprian teaches us to believe only in God. The Church is a body of men, who, however good they may be, are not infallible.' As the result of his enquiries Aulus concludes, 'Why is there such war between you and the orthodox?' and the answer is 'Why indeed?'

In this way Erasmus affirmed his faith, when he seemed about to die. But he did not die. Nine years later death had come nearer, and the world had greatly changed. The schisms which he had feared were becoming accomplished facts—not respectable heresies with the sanction of time behind them, not established differences of use and practice such as the Church was content to allow to the Milanese or the Bohemians. His heart was heavy within him, not for himself but for the troubles that were coming upon the world. Once more he would address the educated audience to whom he had been accustomed to appeal, who had so often looked to him for guidance: though now the clash of faction drowned his failing voice. This is something of what he said:

'How then is schism to be healed? First we must all do our duty—popes and princes, monks and magistrates, priests and laymen, we must all do what lies before us, without ambition or quarrelling, in that spirit of accommodation which makes for concord: only taking care not to compromise away the great foundations of life. We must firmly resolve not to part lightly with the tradition of the past which has been sanctioned by long use and general agreement; and to make no change except under pressure of necessity or for evident benefit. The Freedom of the Will is a thorny question which it profits little to debate; let us leave it to professed theologians. But we can agree that man of his own power can do nothing and is wholly dependent on the mercy of God: that Faith is of great value, a gift of the Holy Spirit, though we may have differences of opinion as to the precise mode of its operation. It is a pious belief that the prayers and good works of the living can help the dead, especially when these have arranged for them beforehand: though it should be remembered that funeral processions and masses instituted only for one's own glorification fail of their reward, and that it is better to spend the money in one's lifetime on good objects. But those who do not share this belief must not mock at the simplicity of others. Again many religious people believe that the Saints have power with God. Those who do not agree should pray direct to Father, Son and Spirit, and must not disturb and vex those who without superstition implore the help of the Saints. Mere superstition, of which I admit there is much in the worship of the Saints, must be refuted; but simple piety may be accepted, even when it is combined with some degree of error. Christ loves simple souls and will hear our vows even if the Saints do not.

'Those who have destroyed the images of the Saints have not acted without reason, though they have perhaps gone too far. Idolatry is a terrible sin: but we can get rid of superstition as it was got rid of in the past, and there is certainly value to be derived from the arts of sculpture and painting, which are a kind of silent poetry. In every house the Life of Christ might be fitly painted on the walls. In churches only sacred subjects should be depicted, of course without any of those unsuitable additions which are only meant to arouse laughter: human subjects, suitably treated, must be confined to cloisters, porches and galleries. Let those who think that images of the Saints, as devoid of any sense, should not be held in honour, enjoy their own thought;

and not disturb others who without superstition lovingly cherish images, as a bride kisses a ring which her husband has sent her or a bracelet which he has left behind.

'So too with those who in the same spirit kiss bones and other relics of the Saints. St. Paul, I think, would let each have his own opinion. One day a man was walking through a graveyard, on a public footpath, and did not take his hat off to a crucifix he passed—not of set purpose, but because he was listening intently to what his companions were saying. A theologian I know, who was looking on, at once exclaimed 'I dare swear that man is a Lutheran'. Now that was wrong: but it is just as wrong to disturb vexatiously the simple religion of those who attach importance to images. We can all surely agree that the best way to worship the saints is to try to imitate their lives.

'Again people who cannot bring themselves to believe that what we now call "Sacramental confession" was instituted by Christ himself may surely agree to preserve it as a valuable practice which has the sanction of long usage. The benefit we derive from it depends largely on ourselves. We can choose our own confessor, who should be honest and intelligent and to be relied upon to hold his tongue. To him we should confess freely as we should to God our open and evident faults, and not by our vague and confused words compel him to extract our sins from us. There must be no superstitious repetition, no minute enumeration of all the circumstances, no flying to another priest in case anything has been forgotten at the first attempt. The great thing is to hate our misdeeds and so to order our lives that we commit no mortal sin. He who can do that has no need of confession. If by accident one slips into sin, one should turn at once to God and make one's peace with him; for confession to a priest a favourable opportunity may be awaited, and to a priest may be referred cases of doubt which arise—about lending money on interest, about marriage, about making restitution, or about the fulfilment of vows. In general, let those who believe that Christ founded confession in its present form, observe it with the utmost care; but they should allow others to retain their own opinions until a Council of the Church has given a definite judgement.

'As for the Mass, any superstition or corruption which has crept in it is reasonable to correct; but why we should find such fault with the whole service I cannot see. It consists of psalmody, the introit, the doxology, prayer and canticles, lessons from the Prophets and from the Apostles and from the Gospels; the Creed, thanksgiving or as it is called the Eucharist, the commemoration of Christ's death, then prayer again, including the Lord's Prayer; after this the symbol of Christian peace, then communion, the sacred canticle and prayer. Finally the priest blesses the people and bids them dwell in unity and godly love. What is there in this which does not arouse reverence? Those who dislike the dirty crowd of hired priests should dismiss the bad ones and keep the good. Details of the service which are displeasing, especially those which are not ancient, may be omitted.

'At Rome to-day the practice of many masses is discouraged. In the Pope's own chapel there is only one altar and one mass; and many churches now follow the Roman usage which forbids private masses, especially while high mass is going on. We must reprove the insolence of those who walk about during mass talking of their own affairs, and then when it is over, go and find a priest of their own to perform a special mass for them: or of others who at vespers seize hold of any priest they meet and compel him even by violence to say separate vespers for them, though he may already have finished his own.

'Some may disapprove of the modern harmonized music and the use of organs. These can quite well be dropped without any loss of piety. But if they are retained, they must be of a kind which is suitable for divine worship, and the rest of the service must not be cut down on their account. These long concerted passages, a single verse often occupying a considerable time, spin out the usual form of service and make it tedious.

'There is superstition also in the multiplicity of masses: the mass of the crown of thorns, the mass of the three nails, the mass of the foreskin of Christ, masses for those who travel by land or by water, for barren women, for women labouring of child, for persons sick of quartan and tertian fevers. Some improvement could be made in these directions: there is no need to abolish the mass altogether.

'Some want to see communion during the mass; as, I admit, Christ ordained and as was formerly the custom. The disappearance of it is due not to the priests but to the laity, who have grown indifferent. That heavenly food is not to be thrust upon the unwilling: it will not be denied to those who ardently desire it. How can there be communion when in many places the churches are almost empty during mass? Some people go out at once after they have been censed and before the introit, others go the moment the Gospel has been read. At the supreme moment of the mass, when the priest is silently giving thanks, each person should be silently communing with God. Instead they stand gossiping in the market-place or sit and drink at a wineshop: which is really less irreverent than the behaviour of people who remain in church but chatter and jest all through the service. Finally, though the priest does not share the sacred elements with the congregation—a practice which was not universally observed, even in antiquity—, they share together the teaching of the Gospels, the exhortation, prayer and praise and thanksgiving.

'Some objections are raised to the adoration in the mass. If Christ is there completely, why should he not be adored? though he is only there in the form of the bread and wine to be received with pure devotion, not to be made a display of at public games or processions, nor to be carried about on horseback through the fields: that is not an ancient practice, but a mere concession to ignorant fancy which ought never to have been made. Some people think themselves very devout if, whenever the priest exhibits the host, they rush up and gaze fixedly upon it. It would be much more religious if they stood afar off like the publican, or prostrated themselves in silent adoration. No one is so stupid as to adore the human instead of the divine nature of Christ, or to worship the bread and wine instead of him. But since no one except the priest himself can know for certain that he has consecrated, the adoration is always subject to a silent condition: yet that which we really adore in Christ is always present with us. Besides if we attend all other sacraments bareheaded, why should anyone object to taking off his hat to this one, even though Christ's body and blood are only there symbolically?'

'Then again, how many different forms there are of sacramentaries! How often the authorities change their own minds about them, or quarrel with the opinions of others! Only recently somebody was impious enough to conceive of a sacrament without any external sign—which is of course essential to a sacrament. People who talk like that have lost all sense of the gravity of the subject. If they really are not clear in their minds, it is much better for them to acquiesce in the belief which the Church has handed down to us from age to age, namely that the true body and blood of Christ are in the Eucharist and without doubt alive. If only we can agree on this, more subtle and intricate questions may be left for the decision of a Council. As it is, the diversity of private opinions turns what should be the comfort and joy of pious souls into something which they almost dislike.

'Of feast days there is a great crowd, which have either been introduced by bishops in deference to popular wish, or invented by popes for no cogent reason: such as the Conception and the Nativity of the Virgin or the Presentation in the Temple. These the authorities will wisely allow to be dropped: and it would not be a bad thing to get rid of all which have no authority in Scripture, always excepting Sunday. There would be no objection to having fewer festivals, if only we keep those which are left more carefully. We need not consider that a day is profaned when a man by honest labour earns enough to support his wife and children or to relieve the wants of his neighbour. But the feasts which private associations have instituted for themselves, are mere occasions for revelry, and should be suppressed with the associations by the magistrates.

'Fasting and special ordinances about food are only enjoined by the Church for health of body and mind; and are not binding on those who cannot stomach fish or who find their vigour diminished by fasting. But when people are all the better for these abstinences, it is mere contumacy to reject useful practices just because they are ordained by the Church. So in this matter we should not judge one another, but let God be our judge. It is the same with all the other Constitutions of the bishops: let us keep those which are good and helpful and not be put off by the name law which is sometimes applied to them.

'I do not wish to lay down the law, nor to dictate to the Church what it ought to do. But while we are waiting for a Council, let us try to remove as many causes of disagreement as we can. We must not do to others what we should dislike for ourselves, nor compel them to new forms of worship which they detest, especially those who shelter themselves behind long established practice. But we might prepare for a Council by attempting some moderate compromise which would be like the syrups which doctors give to prepare the body for some stronger medicine. Only I am afraid that there are some who through lack of judgement or to secure themselves are making haste to inflame the situation, so that a Council will do no good.

'Look at these unhappy Anabaptists: whom I call unhappy, because it is error rather than wickedness that carries them on to their own destruction. Are they not satisfied with baptism as it has been practised in the Church for fourteen hundred years? which in the time of Augustine was so ancient that no one knew its origin, and which the Apostles probably extended to children. Their refusal to obey princes is quite at variance with Christ's command to render unto Caesar the things of Caesar; and the communism they attempt was only possible when the Church was small, and then not among all Christians: as soon as the Gospel spread widely, it became quite impossible. The best way towards agreement is that property should be in the hands of lawful owners, but that out of charity we should share one with another.

'In Bohemia we are told that a new kind of Jews has arisen, called Sabbatarians, who observe the Sabbath so scrupulously that if anything flies into their eye on that day, they will not take it out. As though Christ had not taught us how to keep the Sabbath! Again Paul threatens anathema to even an angel who should bring down from heaven a Gospel other than his own. Now men's minds are so unsteady that any new dogma, however absurd, will find disciples. What can have caused this vacillation among the Germans who have always been distinguished above other nations for courage and constancy?

'How happy should we be if we could lay aside dissensions and dwell with one heart and one mind in the house of the Lord! This is now the care of the great Christian princes—the Emperor, the King of the Romans, the King of France, the King of England, the Pope and his Cardinals; and all other rulers and cities should bend their efforts hither too. We have had enough of quarrels: perhaps sheer weariness may bring us together to concord, to dwell in the house of the Lord as friends. How amiable are thy dwellings, O Lord of Hosts.'

Thus far Erasmus, speaking peace and ensuing it. How far was he qualified to speak for peace? He was an old man when he wrote these words, near sixty-seven. His life had been spent among books, and to no small degree he had become bookish. This was the price he paid, the price all men must pay, for devotion to a cause. No one can consecrate all his energies to a great undertaking without narrowing his field of vision. The process may be either deliberate or unconscious, but the result is the same. The artist builds his studio to catch all the light from the north: east, south, and west he cannot see. Men of action, soldier and sailor, statesman and lawyer, take on gradually the tincture of the work on which they spend their lives: and even more is it so with the men of thought, parson and schoolmaster and don—the windows which should open on all the world get grown over and dimmed with the dust of time, only a few remaining serviceable. For thirty years Erasmus had given himself wholeheartedly to the high task which Colet had opened to him in Oxford—the advancement of sacred learning and the knowledge of God. His faith was unwavering, that in this field above all others man must do his utmost to know, using the abilities and powers that God gives him. His special work had been in divinity, in restoring to their place the Scriptures and the works of the Fathers. The Middle Ages had been content with voluminous commentaries on the Bible, each commentator glossing his predecessor until the sacred text disappeared under the mountains of notes. Erasmus brought men back to the originals, and raised thereby, however faintly and uncertainly, the whole question of the Tradition, that is the study of the means by which the writings of the past are handed down to us, the materials to which they were committed, and the minds and powers of the men who composed and copied them.

This was Erasmus' lifework. His frail little body was often tortured with agony. For his malady, the stone, the surgeons of his day could do little. But after each bout he rose up unflinchingly and returned to his task, and he died at last in harness. Of the amount of work that he achieved it is difficult even for careful students to form a high enough estimate. Small wonder then that he became bookish. In many ways his world was as wide as any man's has ever been. With his great personal charm, wherever he went, he won devoted friends. The highest dignitaries in Western Christendom besought him to come and share their courts; and, failing of their wish to tear the devoted scholar from his books, consulted him incessantly about high matters in Church and State. Popes and bishops urged him to inspire men to godliness, kings asked him to advise. Dwelling thus in a world of his own, above the heads of the masses, it is not surprising that his knowledge of men was limited. With the educated, the intelligent, the right-minded he was at home. He could understand them and they could hear his voice. But with the large sections of mankind to whom reason does not speak—the wicked man going on still in his wickedness, seeking his own and caring for none else; the good man clinging obstinately to error; or that many-headed organism, far larger in his day than in ours, whose eyes are, and must be, holden— in the understanding of all these he was quite at fault, and was inclined to base too much hope on words.

What then is the counsel that Erasmus gives? Agree with one another quickly, and dwell upon the points of your agreement. Define as little as possible, for that way lies division. Make concessions, especially about what may be only matters of individual taste—remembering that things which seem quite intolerable in those we do not like, we can learn to put up with in our friends. His words were useful to the age for which he wrote them: they seem to me just as useful to-day.

ERASMUS' SERVANT-PUPILS

ERASMUS' position and prosperity may be gauged from
the household that he kept. On his first arrival in Paris
in 1495, he entered the College of Montaigu, a plain
Austin Canon. When the rigour of its life drove him
elsewhere, he moved to what seems to have been a kind
of boarding-house. In 1498 we hear of a servant-boy,
whom he proposes to bring with him to stay with the
Lady of Veere at Tournehem; and for whom therefore,
as well as for himself, a horse must be sent. In 1500 he
sends off his boy to the faithful Batt, perhaps in order
to cut down his expenses. The character that he gives
this Louis indicates something of the relation between
this kind of master and servant. 'He is entirely trustworthy which is a great thing in a boy. He writes quickly
and neatly, both in French and Latin. He is fairly well-
educated, painstaking, very obedient, and of quite a
good disposition. He might be useful to you in copying
out books.' In 1506, on his way to Italy, he had a 'minis-
ter' with him in Paris, Gervase Amoenus of Dreux; who
is also called his *discipulus*; so that clearly the boy expected some teaching in return for the service, clerical
and domestic, which he rendered. The nature of such
service may be further illustrated by a letter from the
famous Bishop of Winchester, Stephen Gardiner, written
in ⟨1526⟩ to Erasmus, and inviting him to remember how

'when you were staying at Paris in the house of an Englishman
named Eden in the Rue St Jean, at the time when you first
published the Moria ⟨1511⟩ and were buying a great number of
Greek and Latin books, there was a boy there with Eden, who
every day prepared at your order lettuces cooked with butter
and vinegar, and you used to say you had never had them so

nice anywhere else. I was that boy; and I continually regret that I was so unwise as not to accept the invitation you sent me ⟨in October 1513?⟩ through the Cambridge bookseller, Gerard, to come and be your servant. Then instead of reading your books, I should have had the joy of being taught by you in person.'

At Cambridge in 1513 Erasmus had in his employ a boy named John Smith, son of a Robert Smith, bailiff of the town; the father appears to have been a troublesome character, for the Vice-Chancellor of the University about that time found it necessary to discommons him. To Erasmus, at any rate, the boy's parents were as tiresome as other parents have been known to be. His mother objected to the boy's going abroad; and they were continually changing their minds, saying first one thing and then another. At a crisis which arose after some time, it appears that the objectionable father asked for an interview. Erasmus at once wrote to two of his friends, one of them, Humphrey Walkden, a Fellow of Queens', the college in which Erasmus was living.

'I cannot talk to this beast. I wish you would persuade him that I have been more than a father to the boy, and have looked after his health as well as his education; and that he has not lost his time, but has made more progress than he would have done in any school. If Humphrey can spare the time, I should be glad if he would write something of this sort in English, and send it to me by John to be signed:

'Dear Mr Smith. I have not yet arranged about a servant: for the one whom I regarded as certain, has changed his mind and gone abroad. Still, to comply with your wishes, I am sending John back to you. I have been a father and more than a father to him in everything. This he has deserved, and I do not regret the pains I have taken. He has not completely lost his time. Though his progress may not show at once, he has learnt more Latin than he would have in Wentford's school in three years. I have not beaten him, because he has not deserved it; and high spirited youths are better led than driven. You will perhaps find a better teacher for him, but no one who will love him better in the whole of England.'

A letter at the same time to Wentford, the London schoolmaster mentioned, throws further light:

'The father says the boy doesn't learn, because I don't know English: surely that just compels him to learn Latin whether he will or not. It occurs to me that it is because of my complacence that he has selected me to maintain and teach his son at my own expense. The boy has done less menial work than he would have done in your school. I have treated him handsomely, and he has done no copying for me. I have given him good food and good clothes, and have been diligent in teaching him. If he had been equally eager to learn, he wouldn't now be needing a grammar-master with a birch. I don't say this because I mind about the money; but I resent the father's thinking he can treat me in this way, and then deprive me of my servant without a word of thanks.'

The position was not so desperate as it seemed. John Smith returned to Erasmus, and was allowed to go abroad with him in 1514. At Basle he won golden opinions from the young men in his master's circle, Sapidus, Beatus Rhenanus, Nesen; as later from Morillon at Louvain. From July 1517 to April 1518 he was with Erasmus at Louvain, and copied many of his master's letters into the well-known book now at Deventer; and when at length his mother had her way and got him back to England, Erasmus gave him the warmest commendations and he entered the delightful household of Thomas More.

Two young men who worked with Erasmus at Cambridge, though it is not clear whether they were servant-pupils, were Robert Aldridge, an Eton scholar, and Thomas Lupset, whom Colet sent up from his new school at St. Paul's. Aldridge, who afterwards became Bishop of Carlisle, worked with Erasmus on the text of Seneca

and Jerome from manuscripts in the libraries of Peter-
house and King's: their method of collating these was,
it appears, for one to read aloud while the other followed
—an interesting indication of the standards of scholarly
accuracy at that day. Lupset, who later became one of
Wolsey's lecturers at Oxford, came daily to help Erasmus
in correcting the text of Jerome and the New Testament.
'I help him in return', wrote Erasmus, 'and would gladly
do more, only I do not want to interrupt his studies.'

In the years 1516–18 during which the manuscript
volume already mentioned, his letter-book now at Deventer, was being constructed, four servants can be traced
in his employ, possibly at the same time: a certain John
of Friesland, who left him in September 1517 to seek his
fortune in England; another whose name is not known;
Jacobus Nepos, who went with him to Basle, and settled
there, teaching Greek and working with the printers;
and John Smith. Besides copying for him, they also
carried his letters to and fro across Europe, southwards
to Rome and northwards to England, where so many of
his friends and patrons lived: a service which had now
become of the first importance to him. At Basle he engaged a young man of independent character, John
Hovius, who was not content to remain with him for
long, and later found his fortune in Italy. A letter written
by Hovius, while they were together in the Collège du
Lis at Louvain in 1518–19 gives a picture of their life:
it is addressed to Martin Lypsius, an Austin Canon at
Louvain and a trusted and devoted friend of Eramus—
so that we need not suppose that there was much amiss
in the affair it describes.

'About the paper you sent back,' writes Hovius, 'this is what
happened. Your brother came and knocked at the door, and
when I opened it, handed this in. It chanced that through the

door the Master caught sight of him; and at once he asked
whether there was a letter for him. I said "No"; "What were
you doing with him then?" I hesitated, and then said the worst
thing I could have said, that he had brought back a paper which
I had sent for you to see. At once he blazed up, and would have
slain me almost with his lightnings, that is his smooth sarcasms,
if I hadn't known his ways. Not that he minded your having
seen that; but he declared I had done the same with all the rest.
It was stupid of me not to think of something else to say. So
please keep it to yourself. It is a matter of no consequence, but as
the Master wishes it so, I think I must comply. Burn this letter
and don't let anyone know that I have written to you; and if the
Master comes to see you at any time, don't raise the subject.'

Erasmus on his side found Hovius intractable; 'before
he left, he nearly drove me wild', he wrote later.

In the proud prosperity of his later years Erasmus
gave less and less time to teaching his servants; whose
functions were principally to copy his letters for dispatch
or to carry them to their destinations, doing also other
business for him. Side by side with them we find other
young men, coming to crave permission to dwell in his
house, not as servants but as paying guests, for the
pleasure of such shreds of his company as he could spare
them. In the former class may be mentioned Livinus
Goethals of Ghent, no doubt of the family to which
belonged the great quodlibetarian. This name, for convenience in finding a classical dress, Erasmus transformed into Algoet, Panagathus, or Omnibonus. He was
a boy with little force of character, who drifted through
life hoping for more than he deserved; but the following
letter, written from Antwerp during a short visit from
Louvain, shows the busy scholar and the friend of kings
in a pleasing and paternal light.

'My return is delayed for some days; so I write to repeat what
I told you when I was starting. Do not be lazy over your books

because I am away: you ought rather to be more active, for you are now released from your customary duties. Indeed it was just for this that I left you behind: so do not let me be disappointed when I come back. Avoid bad company, and stick close to Carinus: he is not much older than you, but his example and his enthusiasm for study will be a great help to you. You have good natural abilities, and you owe it to your parents and to the Dean of Bruges who commended you to me like a father, to make good use of them. I have always treated you more as a son than a servant; and people will expect much from you for having lived in my household. You have everything you can want to smooth your way; money enough, and plenty of books and teachers; and at Louvain you are surrounded by boys and young men who are all doing their utmost to learn Latin and Greek. Besides you have a name that you must live up to.

'I write in this way not because I doubt your application, but because I am so eager that you should do your best. If any letters come which seem of no great importance, keep them till my return. But if there are any which are urgent, and no convenient messenger arrives, bring them over here yourself.'

Others who carried Erasmus' letters were Charles Harst from the neighbourhood of Spires, afterwards an important executive officer in the service of the Duke of Cleves. He joined Erasmus in 1524, and in 1525 executed an important mission to Rome, to obtain for his master papal permission to make a will: a man whom he trusted greatly. For eight or nine years Erasmus was served by Quirinus Talesius of The Hague, who met a cruel death as burgomaster of Haarlem in 1573, on suspicion of communication with the Spaniards. Another messenger was Nicholas Cannius of Amsterdam, a friend of his fellow townsmen Alard and Cornelius Crocus. After supplying one of the characters to Erasmus' colloquy *Cyclops*, in which he is supposed to have afforded cover for some jests at Oecolampadius, he returned to Holland in

1529–30 to end his days as rector of a house of Ursulines in Amsterdam and parish priest.

The servant of Erasmus' later years to whom he was most closely attached was Gilbert Cousin or Cognatus of Nozeroy in the Franche-Comté, who later played some part in the reformation of his native county and endured persecution. He left Erasmus in 1535 to perform the duties of a canonry to which he had been appointed; but he showed his devotion to the Master and his pride in the service to which he had been admitted, by having a woodcut drawn (in 1533?) showing himself writing at Erasmus' dictation; while between them on the table stands the vase of flowers which Erasmus loved to have before him. To Cognatus we owe a view of a servant's life and duties in a small treatise Οἰκέτης, which Oporinus printed for him at Basle in 1535. A servant's virtues are, he considers, to be trusty in everything, in doing as well as in not peeping or listening, speedy in going his ways, and lowly in his own eyes. Incidentally he tells us that Englishmen keep too many servants: he has a story of a rogue who insinuated himself into the household of a Polish bishop and got his meat for long without detection among so many others; and he ends with an explanation of the quaint figure so familiar to all Wykehamists, which he describes as of French origin. Another view of the young servant-pupil's life may be read in a letter of Erasmus discussing in 1529 the future of the young John Erasmius Froben, his godson, who since the death of his father the printer had been, as he considered, neglected, or at least mismanaged by his relatives. The boy was now about fourteen, and Erasmus had taken him into his own house from another establishment where he had been ill placed: 'When I took pity on him he was the only pupil there to have any teaching, and he got a fair share of beating. He waited at table, where there were six boarders and no servant kept. He also helped in the kitchen and carried water for the whole house.'

A service that Erasmus regularly required of his young men was to read aloud to him. He liked to walk up and down after his meals: in a garden in the afternoon, after supper in his room; and as he did so, his servant would sit and read to him from a book. The management of Erasmus' kitchen seems to have been left to a woman of discreet age, who was no doubt within her own dominion supreme and ruled the household with a rod of iron. Her ascendancy is reflected in a sentence of one of his letters to Boniface Amerbach: 'You are wise to be staying with Glareanus and not with me. My maid-servant is rancid to-day.'

After returning to Basle in 1521 Erasmus began to receive into his house young men of quite a different type: rich men furnished with ability, who caught at the opportunity of living for a time in such charming and distinguished company, and were willing to pay well for the privilege: not of course rendering any service to their host, but living under his roof and sharing his table. Even while he was still dwelling with Froben in the house Zum Sessel, we hear of a *conuiua*, one Louis Carinus of Lucerne, who had been the pupil of his friends Glareanus and Nesen earlier. Then in October 1522 he settled into a big house on the Nadelberg above Froben's but with their courtyards communicating; and there for six years and a half he kept the state of a potentate, so far as it was possible for one who was always, as he termed it, 'working at the mill'. The first *conuiua* that we hear of is Crato Stalberger, of a wealthy Frankfort family, who also had been a pupil of Nesen, and who had become

Doctor of Medicine at Antwerp. In 1524 came Sigismund Gelenius, a learned Bohemian, who was the prop and stay of the Frobens' firm for nearly twenty years after Erasmus' death. In one of the later volumes he edited for them, a Symmachus in 1549, he recalls with happy memory the delightful days he had spent with Charles Harst twenty-five years before under Erasmus' roof, and their conversations carried far into the night. The winter of 1524–5 brought Francis Dilft of Antwerp, a young man for whom Erasmus always had a tender affection. Three or four times he came in the next years, and each time stayed for several months: once we hear of him obligingly journeying from Freiburg to Besançon to fetch the Burgundy wine on which the Master's health depended. The hopes Erasmus formed of him were justified by his becoming Imperial Ambassador to the Court of London in his last years.

A more important visitor was John Lasky, second son of a Palatine of Sieradz in Poland, afterwards to be famous in the history of the English Reformation as John Alasco. In May 1524 he came with his elder brother to Basle, and was at once captivated by the personality of Erasmus. When his brother's embassy to Paris was finished, they came back through Basle, and there John was left behind, to dwell for nearly a year in these happy surroundings. The attraction between master and pupil which Erasmus frequently asserts is corroborated by Beatus Rhenanus in dedicating to the young Pole some notes on Pliny's *Natural History* in 1526. Lasky's generous nature quickly showed itself. Besides undertaking the whole cost of the kitchen while he was under Erasmus' roof, he also refurnished some part of the house; and in June 1525 he contracted to buy Erasmus' library, on the handsome terms that though paying half the purchase money at once, he should allow the Master to retain the books until his death. In 1537 the contract was duly fulfilled and the books went off to Poland, where few, if any, of them can now be traced. A brief note from him to Boniface Amerbach shows something of what life was like in the house Zur alten Treue on the Nadelberg: 'Yesterday when I was playing my usual game after supper for exercise, I chanced to hit my great toe against a stone: so I cannot struggle upstairs to see Erasmus without great difficulty. Unless you are kind enough to come and help me, I am afraid nothing will be done in my brother's business: but I am sure you will.'

ERASMUS' RELATIONS WITH HIS PRINTERS

MOST of us probably can recall something of the sensations with which we first saw ourselves in print. A boy reading his name for the first time in his school magazine feels to have stepped upon the stage of the world and become almost a public personage: as though all eyes that passed over the important page could not but be rivetted upon initials and letters which to him seem so familiar. And when first he sees in print something of his own composition, what a wonderful adventure! the halting sentences are transfigured with dignity by their appearance in type, until, as he reads, he feels almost as though an oracle had spoken.

If such thoughts can arise now, what must it have been when the art of printing was young! In the days of hireling scribes, ploughing out their work with no guarantee of uniformity, a budding author might allow himself ten or twenty copies of some composition, for presentation to patrons and friends; hoping that admiration might win for it wider existence. But if once he could persuade a printer to accept his work, his name might travel, whilst he slept, into all lands, from the borders of the 'uncombed Russians' to the new dominions that a united Spain was founding across the Western seas. To a reputation for elegance he might add the credit of being modern and progressive, not a mere runner after novelties, but ready to profit by man's great inventions which had 'come to stay'. Hence it is that by 1500 we find many names, often otherwise quite unknown, beside that of the author in the opening and closing pages of books. Friends present verses or letters of compliment, and he has not the heart nor the wish to deny them; dependents of the

patron to whom he has dedicated his book, force their
way in with similar effusions; even the printer's correctors struggle to get a mention. The art of self-advertise-
ment—which is not without its uses and temptations
even to-day—had thus received a new development, for
those that had the wits to make use of it.

Erasmus was above all things quick-witted. The first
glimpses that we have of him show him as dissatisfied
with his surroundings, and catching at every opportunity
to make his way out into a larger sphere. As the younger
son of a poor parish priest, with both parents dead before
he had reached nineteen, his entry into life was far less
fortunate than that of youths who claimed a bishop or
a cardinal as father. His early years were not devoid of
movement. From the town school of his native Gouda
he went off as a singing-boy to the cathedral of Utrecht,
under the famous musician Obrecht; and along its aisles
—not yet so cruelly severed from the fine western tower
—we may picture him in red cassock and lace-trimmed
surplice playing pranks with all the audacious impishness
of an *enfant de chœur*. Then for a long while, possibly nine
years, he was at Deventer, one of the great schools of the
age; and for the most part of his time there was immersed
in the formal studies of the Middle Ages, until Hegius,
who had learnt Greek from Agricola, came to be head
master in 1483, and brought a breath of something
better. A year later he left school, no doubt because of
an outbreak of plague. He was hoping to make his way
to the University: but his father died, and his guardians
found no means left to gratify this wish. The best they
could do was to find places for the boys in a seminary
at Hertogenbosch in Brabant, kept by the Brethren
of the Common Life; and there two more years were
spent. At the end Erasmus returned home to Gouda,

to see little prospect of help from any quarter. After
a period of dejection he drifted into a monastery which
lay a mile outside the town; a house of Augustinian
canons at Steyn. The attraction which drew him thither
was certainly not the cloister rule. He was a religious
man, but ever too original and independent to order his
life at the command of others. It was rather that some
possibility of study had been shown to him. Within the
walls he might look for maintenance and leisure. The
spirit of the Renaissance was stirring in the North, and
he had caught the infection. These beloved studies might
lead him he knew not whither. The religious orders were
powerful, and to a learned ecclesiastic many doors were
open. But after two years he was still at Steyn, reading
the classics and the Fathers, everything he could lay his
hands on, amongst companions of whom some were
openly disapproving, others stolidly apathetic; his only
comfort a friend or two who could make some pretence
of sharing his tasks, provided that he was not too insis-
tent with them.

Dutchmen are rightly proud of their country, and
Erasmus was no exception. In after years, though he
never proposed to settle there again, he wrote of it with
enthusiasm, as a land which lacked nothing of the conditions which make for cultivated and refined existence:
attributing this to the great estuaries into which the
stately ships could bring the wares of all the markets of
the world, to be distributed again along its navigable
rivers; praising its birds and fish, its groves and rich
meadows.[1] But for all that it is a flat land, offering little
variety to refresh the mind, unless perhaps an occasional
church tower, standing guardian among the great fens,
and only visible at intervals through gaps in distant

[1] *Adag.* 3535: Auris Bataua.

fringes of trees. This is how an English visitor[1] writes
of the now ill-famed island of Walcheren, thirty years
later than the period we are considering. After complaining of the peat-smoke in the towns, which pervades
everything and fills nose and chest and head, he goes on:
'If you wish to take a walk in the country the roads are
so slimy that the least shower of rain renders progress
difficult; and you cannot turn into the fields because of
the deep ditches which cut you off on either side. The
only pleasant place to walk is on the dykes beside the
sea; but to get there you must pass hundreds of flax-
pools, which smell worse than any drain. And as you
must return the same way, they drive out any pleasure
you have had, and send you home again dull and sad.'
Such was the land in which Erasmus' life was cast, in the
petty circle of which the house at Steyn was the centre.
By the time he was twenty-three, he had scarcely seen a
hill, except the low eminences at Arnhem on his way to
and from Deventer, and had perhaps never set his foot
'where the broad ocean leans against the land'. At the
age when our undergraduates have finished their course,
he was pining for a university, Louvain or Cologne or the
distant dignities of Paris. To his pent spirit, beating its
wings against the bars and eager to be flown, the ships
that later he could extol must have brought only bitterness. They could spread their sails and be gone adown
the breeze: but for him it seemed the breeze would never
blow. The Rhine that bore them forth had come from
the snowy Alps, and beyond was the sweet realm of Italy,
the Holy City and its famed river:[2] but his foot was
chained, like a hobbled pony's, to the low lands in which

---

[1] Tunstall in 1517: see Erasmus, *Ep.* 663.
[2] Cf. Ode 2 in the *Sylua Odarum* of his friend and companion at
Steyn, William Herman.

he had been born, far away from the great centres of
intellectual life.

At length an opportunity came, and the young canon
was quick to seize it. In the autumn of 1489 Gerard Leeu,
the well-known Gouda printer, was on a visit to his home.
Five years before he had moved his press to the more
flourishing centre of Antwerp; and now, perhaps, having
loaded his packs upon the barges that would carry them
up the Rhine to the great fair at Frankfort, he had come
away for a holiday to see his friends. One of the books
that he brought with him was the curious fourth-century
Christian cento, composed out of Virgil by Falconia
Proba, wife of a Roman magnate, and dedicated to the
Emperor Honorius. This had been edited for Leeu,
12 September 1489, by James Canter of Groningen, a
member of an erudite Friesland family, and brother of
an infant prodigy who at the age of ten had been sum-
moned to Vienna for the Emperor to see. Many of Leeu's
books have plenty of room upon the title-page. In
Proba's cento it is absolutely blank, and the book begins
on the verso with Canter's prefatory letter. A copy came
into Erasmus' hands, possibly on the autumn morning as
he walked down with Leeu to the ferry where the printer
was to cross the Yssel on his return to Antwerp. Clearly
here was a chance. A florid eulogy of the editor and the
printer would do well for the front page, if Leeu could be
persuaded to add it in a new issue, or in later copies of
the present one. Just such an effusion[1] Erasmus composed, in the form of a letter to Canter, and dispatched
it to Antwerp: but it seems to have been too late. The
book was perhaps not successful enough to justify a
second issue. At any rate the letter has not been traced
earlier than Merula's volume of 1607, printed from a

[1] *Ep.* 32.

collection of manuscripts some of which were in Erasmus' autograph, and which included a great many letters, probably in an album, which belong to the period of his residence at Steyn.

I should make it clear that the statements made above rest partly on inference. The letter exists, and the book exists: but that Erasmus wished to combine one with the other is only a suggestion. There is, however, some colour for this in his action a few years later in Paris. The bird had made his way, then, out of the cage. His evident talents could not be hid, for he could write Latin with greater facility than any one around him. A powerful bishop wanted a secretary to go with him to Rome, where he hoped to be made a cardinal. Erasmus heard of the post—this seems more likely than that the bishop should have heard of Erasmus—applied for it, and so escaped from his monastery into the great world. After a while the bishop abandoned his project, but his secretary was still on his hands. Being of a kindly disposition he wished to solace the young man for his disappointment about Rome, and so promised to let him go and take a degree in Paris.

By the autumn of 1495 Erasmus was in residence. He speedily set about making his name known. With a polite copy of verses he courted the acquaintance of Gaguin, General of the Mathurins, the leader of the literary world in Paris, an old-fashioned and respectable figure. Fortune favoured him. Gaguin had composed a *History of France*, a work of some magnitude: but while the book was coming through the press, its author fell ill and could take little part in the supervision. At the end, the printer, Peter le Dru, found that he had not enough material to fill his last sheet. Though he spaced out with great amplitude the complimentary verses that had

come in, there was a whole folio blank. An Austin canon
who was studying at Montaigu College, offered a fluent
panegyric on Gaguin, praising the style 'as elegant as
Sallust, as felicitous as Livy', the graphic narrative, the
arrangement and compression of material; and exhorting
France to embrace this immortal monument and its
author. There was enough and to spare: only by squeez-
ing could it be accommodated on the two pages available.
At the head came the writer's name—the earliest authen-
tic form in which it is found—Herasmus Roterdam.[1] He
had been right in estimating the value of the advertise-
ment. Four years later, when he went to Oxford, Colet
could pay him the compliment of saying that his name
had long been familiar:[2] since he had read the letter with
admiration as he passed through Paris, *c.* 1496.

Before long Erasmus persuaded a printer, Antony
Denidel, to undertake a volume of his own: twelve leaves
of poems, entitled *De casa natalitia Iesu*,[3] and containing
also some hymns and a pastoral in which he flattered
without measure Gaguin's History and the Eclogues of
Faustus Andrelinus, an Italian of rather questionable
character, who had then some vogue in the university.
Of this very rare volume I have only heard of two copies,
one in the British Museum, and the other beyond our
reach at Cracow. Next year, just about the same time,
he induced Guy Marchand to bring out a larger volume
of poems by William Herman, his school-friend at Gouda
and companion at Steyn:[4] adding at the end one of his
own, also addressed to Gaguin, in which he complained
sadly of the ill fortune that seemed to dog him at every
step. The thought in his mind was no doubt his disappointment about Italy.

His next venture was after his visit to England in 1499–

---

[1] Erasmus, *Ep.* 45.   [2] *Ep.* 106.   [3] *Ep.* 47.   [4] *Ep.* 49.

1500: a volume of *Adagiorum Collectanea*, designed to help aspirants to elegance in Latin composition. For this he selected a new publisher, John Philippi of Kreuznach, who had just set up his second press in Paris. From the letters of this period it appears that Erasmus took some responsibility for the sale; for he sent copies about to different friends to be disposed of,[1] as many as 100 to England.[2] Philippi also published his next book, some notes on Cicero's *De Officiis*; another very rare volume of which I know only two copies, at Schlettstadt[3] and at Wolfenbüttel. Erasmus' preface[4] for it is dated 28 April ⟨1501⟩; but by the time the printing was near completion, the plague broke out in Paris and he fled off to Holland, leaving the book to look after itself. Philippi gave it a charming title-page, but seems to have forgotten the preface; which was not printed till 1519, when Erasmus edited the *De Officiis* again.

He was now away from Paris and his printers there for three years, 1501–4. The last two of these were spent at Louvain, where he came into contact with Thierry Martens and began a connexion which lasted for many years. Martens had succeeded to Leeu's press at Antwerp in 1493, had come to Louvain in 1498, and now in 1502 was on the point of moving back from the university town to the centre of commerce. As in Paris, so too here Erasmus began with a complimentary letter[5] for a treatise by a friend, James Anthonisz of Middelburg, who had been Vicar-general to his episcopal patron: but this time the letter, instead of being squeezed into the last page to serve the printer's need, received the place of honour at the beginning. The book appeared on 1 April 150⅔, and with another notable change; for the name Erasmus

---

[1] *Epp.* 135, 138, 142, 172.   [2] *Epp.* 129, 181.
[3] Cat. Rhen. 966.   [4] *Ep.* 152.   [5] *Ep.* 173.

appears here for the first time without its H. Martens
took a liking to the ecclesiastic, whose fame was now
growing; and printed two books for him during this
period, the *Lucubratiunculae*,[1] containing the *Enchiridion
militis Christiani*,[2] 15 February 150¾, and a Panegyric,[3]
s.a., addressed to the Archduke Philip, who had just
returned from visiting Spain. For the printing of the
latter volume Erasmus went to Antwerp, and worked in
Martens' office; again filling up the last sheet by a complimentary letter[4] to a friend. For some years Martens
and Erasmus did not meet. The printer remained at
Antwerp till 1512, when he returned to Louvain; the
scholar divided his time between Paris, Italy, and England, with only one brief visit to the Netherlands. But
they were naturally attracted to one another. In the
summer of 1514, when Erasmus was setting out for his
first visit to Basle, he passed through Antwerp and
Louvain. In the last ten years his position had greatly
changed. From a scholar of slight reputation, at whose
works printers looked with hesitancy, he had become a
leader in the world of letters, whose projects were discussed in anticipation, and who could make his own
terms. After he had passed on southwards, a friend wrote
to him from Louvain:[5] 'Martens wishes to be commended
to you. He was very eager to see you, and would have
entertained you in his house. He went to Antwerp to
meet you, but finding that you had come on here, he
turned back at once, and walking all through the night,
arrived at Louvain an hour and a half after you had
left. He will do anything to serve you, and is your most
devoted friend.' Business no doubt played some part
in Martens' activity, which for a man of over sixty was

[1] *Ep.* 93.   [2] *Ep.* 164.   [3] *Ep.* 179.
[4] *Ep.* 180.   [5] *Ep.* 304, 148–156.

remarkable. He would have been glad enough to print some of the books which Erasmus was known to have in hand. But we may also give some credit to human affection: for four years later when Erasmus returned to Louvain suffering from what was thought to be the plague, Martens received him into his house and nursed him for a month till he was well[1]—an action of 'sincere friendship' which surely could hardly be transcended.

In 1504 Erasmus returned to France. Philippi reprinted the little book of *Adagia* for him; but that was their last transaction together. For in the interval since his departure a new press had been set up in Paris, by the enterprising and scholarly Badius Ascensius, the pupil of Trechsel at Lyons. To him Erasmus committed an important manuscript he had brought back from the Abbey of Parc, near Louvain, Valla's Annotations on the New Testament ;[2] and the book was completed by April 1505, before Erasmus' second visit to England. Badius' books had not yet arrived at the handsome title-pages which mark his later works, from 1507 onwards, with ever-increasing richness of design. But in some respects the technical execution was already at a high state of excellence: so that there was good reason for Erasmus to be satisfied. Badius on his side was scholar enough to realize the character of the work offered to him. In consequence he readily undertook more of Erasmus' books; the translations from Euripides[3] and Lucian[4] which Erasmus brought with him on his way to Italy in 1506, a slightly enlarged edition of the *Adagiorum Collectanea* with some *Epigrammata* added in 1506–7, and a reprint of Martens' edition of the Panegyric.

In October 1507, at the end of his first year in Italy, Erasmus determined to make approaches to the printer

---

[1] *Ep.* 867, 195–249.   [2] *Epp.* 182, 3.   [3] *Ep.* 188.   [4] *Ep.* 187.

whose fame then eclipsed all others, Aldus Manutius. He
was projecting a visit to Rome at Christmas time,[1] and
wished to have some volume to take with him for presentation to patrons whom he might design to court. So he
proposed to Aldus a new issue of the translations from
Euripides.

'Badius' venture has been quite successful', he writes,[2] 'for
he has sold every copy. But there are a great number of mistakes; so that though he offers a new edition in which these
should be set right, I am not confident of the result. If you
would undertake the work as a matter of business, I should feel
secure of immortality. In your fine small type (the italic) it will
make only a tiny book and cost very little. On these terms I
would make no charge for the corrected copy (of Badius' edition)
sent with this, and ask only for a few presentation volumes. If
I were staying longer in Italy, I would undertake it at my own
cost and risk; but I must be going in a few months. However,
if you would prefer it, I will engage to take one or two hundred
copies, at a fair price: though I am not good at such trading,
and a parcel of books will be rather a burden to drag about
with me.'

For more than a year Aldus' press had been at a stand-
still, by reason of the wars which were harassing Italy:
not a volume appeared in 1506, and this of Erasmus' was
the only production of 1507. Erasmus' next letter shows
that Aldus undertook it at his own risk; for it asks for
twenty or thirty copies to be sent as soon as finished, and
offers to pay for them in advance or at once on receipt.[3]
Other points raised in the letter are of interest. It appears
to have been proposed that the volume should contain
a complimentary letter from Erasmus to Aldus, and some
sort of reply in the form of a dedication from the printer.
In both matters Erasmus gave him a free hand. 'If the
letter seems too long, I have underlined some passages

---

[1] *Ep.* 209, 44–6.   [2] *Ep.* 207, 26–44.   [3] *Ep.* 209, 49–52.

which you may omit.' 'I shall be glad of your testimony;
but if there is anyone else to whom you can render a
service in this way, do just as you like.' In the translation
he invites Aldus to correct evident mistakes, and even
to make more disputable changes if he had a clear view:
but typographical accuracy the author felt to be no part
of his own responsibility. 'You will probably find a
number of printer's errors: please have a sharp lookout
kept for these.'

Another matter shows him in a less agreeable light.
Badius' edition had contained a copy of verses in praise
of Erasmus by Gervasius Amoenus of Dreux, who had
been his servant during his two months' residence in
Paris in the summer of 1506. Aldus was instructed to
omit it: 'I told the boy in joke that his verses should
appear, and to carry on the deception handed the paper
to Badius, just as I was leaving. Why he printed it I can't
imagine; for I had told him that I only wanted to make
fun of the boy by letting him hope for this.' Rather a
cruel joke it sounds now; but to the taste of that age it
was probably regarded as a neat and clever trick.

This first transaction over Euripides led to an invitation to Erasmus to come and visit the Neacademia.
After being kept waiting at the door because the servant
knew him not and took him for a mere sightseer, he soon
came to an agreement with Aldus for the publication of
a much larger volume than anything he had as yet composed, the *Adagiorum Chiliades*. For eight or nine months
he dwelt with Andrew Asulanus, in considerable discom-
fort, as he afterwards revealed, but working indefatigably
to keep pace with the compositors. Then at Christmas,
1508, he left and went South, to Siena and Rome. Next
summer when he was hurrying back to England to profit
by the opening of the new reign, he had some composition

that he wished Aldus to print;[1] but he had no time to turn aside to Venice, and nothing came of his proposal.

He was never in Italy again, and before long Aldus died. But his connexion with the firm through Andrew and Francis Asulanus, father and son, continued most amicable. In 1515–16 they reprinted his *Moria* and the translations from Lucian, and in 1517 he was proposing to send them other of his compositions, probably a new edition of the *Adagia*:[2] which was, however, in the end given to Froben. In February 1518 the Aldine New Testament was dedicated to Erasmus;[3] and in 1526 they sent him the handsome present of their *editio princeps* of Galen[4] in five volumes: although in the interval there had been passages between author and printers over new editions of the *Adagia*—a work to which they seemed to consider they had some priority of claim, in consequence of the edition of 1508. Later on Erasmus' feelings towards them became somewhat acerbated. In March 1531 Julius Caesar Scaliger, in defending Ciceronianism and its hero against Erasmus' quite good-natured criticism, made a savage attack upon the Dutchman's life at Venice in 1508, accusing him of gross feeding and heavy drinking and other disagreeable habits. Erasmus was stung into a hasty reply, and cooled his wrath by lampooning not Scaliger but Andrew Asulanus in the colloquy *Opulentia sordida*, which first appeared in September 1531. He had one real grudge against Venice. It was there that he had first learnt the agonies of stone:[5] and these he attributed in his mind to the bad wine he had drunk month after month at Asulanus' board. Now, twenty-three years later, his delicate frame was almost

---

[1] de Nolhac: *Corresp. d'Alde Manuce*, p. 84.
[2] *Epp.* 588, 51–4; 589, 30–6.   [3] *Ep.* 770.
[4] *Ep.* 1746.   [5] de Nolhac, *Erasme en Italie*, p. 107.

worn out by the accumulated sufferings of a lifetime: and to be accused of guttling and guzzling, he who had been under- rather than over-fed by the friend who should have nourished him well as part of the price of his services, was more than he could bear. So, probably in a few hours, he dashed off a picture of what life had been to him during those months when he had been toiling over the great book which had made his fame—the meals few and unpunctual, the food scanty and scarcely fit to eat, the wine so sour and thick that it made him ill. The colloquy is obviously overdrawn and reads maliciously now; one wishes it had not been written. But in that age much that we think offensive was tolerated in the name of humour. There is reason to believe that the Venetian circle took no exception to the skit, though the disguise is thin and easily penetrated. At any rate Baptista Egnatius writes to Erasmus a few years later in complete friendliness.[1]

After his return to England Erasmus produced very little for two or three years. In spite of the strictures quoted above in the letter to Aldus—which from their position must not be taken too seriously—he resumed relations with Badius. The *Moria*, which was perhaps too audacious for so serious a printer, was given to Gilles Gourmont, afterwards famous for his printing of Greek.[2] But a more substantial work, *De copia verborum ac rerum*,[3] was readily accepted by Badius, together with a new edition of Lucian and some notes on Seneca[4]; and at the same time he plucked up courage to print the *Moria*, which within six months of its first appearance had been quickly and no doubt profitably reprinted by Schurer at Strasburg and Martens at Antwerp. But he was hoping for greater things. When Erasmus came to Paris in 1511,

----

[1] LB., 1272.   [2] *Ep.* 222.   [3] *Ep.* 260.   [4] *Ep.* 263, 2 n.

there was already talk of a new edition of the *Adagia*.[1]
This Badius expected to secure, as well as an edition of
Jerome's Letters, on which Erasmus was known to have
been long engaged. Badius' letter of 19 May 1512 is
valuable as giving the prices he was prepared to offer, in
addition probably to maintenance, if Erasmus should
choose to come to Paris and see the books through the
press: 15 florins had been agreed upon for the *Adagia*,
and he offers 3 more for the copy, presumably one of the
Aldine volumes with corrections by Erasmus; 15 florins
for Jerome and 15 more for the *Copia* and the other works
which were just come,[2]—48 florins in all. Some years
later Erasmus tells us that he paid Froben 15 gold pieces
(= 20 florins) a month for his board and lodging at
Basle:[3] so that Badius' offer amounted to a sum which
would have kept Erasmus for two months and a half.

But Badius was doomed to disappointment: the *Adagia*
and Jerome were to go elsewhere. The negotiations with
him had been conducted through Francis Berckman, a
Cologne bookseller, who had an office at Antwerp, and
was accustomed to travel to and fro between England,
France, Switzerland, and the Low Countries in pursuit
of his business; acting regularly as carrier of letters and
parcels from one country to another, and arranging payments of money. Like other go-betweens he often disappointed both sides, and in consequence had a reputation
which he perhaps did not wholly deserve. The revised
edition of Erasmus' *Adagia* had been preparing for Badius
during 1512, and the preface[4] is dated 5 January 1513.
In December 1513, Erasmus writes to a friend as follows:[5]

'The booksellers have treated me very badly about the *Adagia*.
Somebody at Basle has printed it as a complete counterfeit of the

---

[1] *Ep.* 219, 3. [2] *Ep.* 263, 36–9. [3] *Ep.* 1528.
[4] *Ep.* 269. [5] *Ep.* 283, 152–64.

Aldine volume. I gave the new copy to Berckman to hand over to Badius or anyone else that Badius should recommend. With his usual honesty he took it straight to Basle to this new printer: who will sit upon it for ten years, I expect, until he has sold off his present issue. I gave Berckman some additions to Plutarch and Lucian for Badius, too: but these have probably gone to Basle like the rest. However I have another copy of the *Adagia* left: so I can be even with him.'

This does not sound like genuine indignation. I have little doubt but that Erasmus had arranged for the transfer. He knew that Badius had not enough Greek type[1] for the *Adagia*, much less for the New Testament which was also in hand: so that it was an evident advantage to get into touch with a firm of such resources and renown as Amorbach and Froben at Basle, the latter being the printer of whom Erasmus affects scarcely to have heard. It is worth noting that on the title-page of Froben's 'counterfeit' edition was an appreciative eulogy of Erasmus, who had been ill in the summer of 1513 and was rumoured throughout Europe to have died. Such words may have influenced Erasmus' decision, if the scales of choice were at all evenly balanced. The decision brought together the greatest scholar and the greatest printer in Transalpine Europe—a connexion that was only severed by death.

But before we follow Erasmus to Basle, mention must be made of the one book that he gave to make its first appearance from an English press: a translation from Plutarch addressed to John Yonge, the Master of the Rolls.[2] According to the English custom[3] he presented it to his patron on 1 January 1513, but later in the year it was printed by Pynson, 28 July 1513, *non omnino inuenuste*.[4] This volume also is very rare: but in December

---

[1] *Epp.* 264, 17–21; 815, 1.   [2] *Ep.* 268.
[3] *Cat. Lucub.*, p. 8, 7–8.   [4] *Ep.* 273, 5.

1910, one was brought to my notice in the University Library at Freiburg, by Dr. Bruno Claussen, who was then assistant there, and another has been acquired by the British Museum.

In July 1514, Erasmus at length set out for Basle, carrying with him the fruits of five years' work in London and at Cambridge—the letters of Jerome, a new translation of the New Testament into Latin and a volume of Annotations, a revised text of Seneca, and lesser compositions. As he passed through Louvain he left behind for Martens—whom, as we saw above, he just missed— a little book of the *Disticha* attributed to Cato and other moral writings.[1] At Strasburg he had a great reception. The burgomasters called upon him, the Literary Society paid him every attention;[2] Schurer secured permission to add on the title-page of a new edition of the *De ratione studii*,[3] 'ex recognitione autoris, dum mense Augusto Argentinae degeret, MDXIIII'. This printer, who was M.A. of Cracow, had since 1509 been reprinting Erasmus' *Adagiorum Collectanea* almost every year; possibly with his permission, for they probably met in July or August 1509, when Erasmus passed through Strasburg on his way back from Italy and may have seen Schurer's first issue which appeared in July, and the page on which the printer lauded him as 'Germanorum omnium eloquentissimus Latinissimusque'. To so faithful an admirer were now entrusted the *Parabolae*[4] which were to appear for the first time, and a revised edition of the *De Copia*.[5] At Schlettstadt his welcome was equally honorific. The town council sent to his lodging three large flagons of wine—the customary offering to distinguished strangers —and bade him to dine next day; and the headmaster

---

[1] *Ep.* 298.   [2] *Ep.* 305.   [3] *Ep.* 66, introd.
[4] *Ep.* 312.   [5] *Ep.* 311.

of the famous school rode with him the last stages of his
way to Basle. The story of his introduction of himself to
Froben—John Amorbach was now dead—has often been
told from his own words:[1] how he marched in pretending
to be Erasmus' plenipotentiary, proffering a letter in the
scholar's own hand; and how when he gave the hint that
revealed him to them, old Lachner ran off to the inn, paid
his reckoning, and brought back his horse and luggage,
that he might be their guest. The University at once
fêted him; and from long distances scholars journeyed
into Basle to see him.

If his thoughts turned back twenty-five years, it must
have seemed a wonderful contrast: the young friendless
canon penned up in the walls of Steyn and trying every
shift that might open a prospect before him, was now
rapidly becoming the dictator of literary Europe, for
whose work printers in all lands were ready to compete.
He found the Plutarch that Berckman had secured the
year before already in the press; at least it appeared in
August 1514, and he did not arrive till after the 15th.[2]
The *Adagia* was quickly put in hand,[3] to the confusion
of his prognostications quoted above: Jerome found its
place in the edition which John Amorbach had long been
projecting;[4] and then Seneca followed.[5] Only the New
Testament remained. This, as requiring abundance of
Greek type, he may have destined for Aldus. When he
first arrived in Basle, his intention was to stay only a
month, and then go on to Italy.[6] But Basle was attractive, and Froben's circle delightful: most important of
all, the resources of Froben's press were equal to any
enterprise. He lingered on, working at great pressure;
and spring found him still North of the Alps, with no

---

[1] *Ep.* 305, 179 *seq.*   [2] *Ep.* 301, 44 n.   [3] *Ep.* 305, 222.
[4] *Ep.* 396.   [5] *Ep.* 325.   [6] *Ep.* 300, 40–1.

decision as to who should print the New Testament. In March he made a rapid visit to England on business, and also to look up points in the manuscripts of Jerome he had used.[1] Meanwhile Aldus had died;[2] so that there was more reason why Erasmus should listen to Froben's offers.[3] At length a bargain was struck, but little progress was made before the autumn.[4] In May 1516 he was able to return to England with the knowledge that the New Testament was out and that Jerome was on its way to completion: the *Adagia*, Seneca, a revised edition of the *Moria*, and other smaller works having already appeared in 1515.

The experience of these two seasons in Basle cemented the friendship which had so auspiciously begun. From this time onward Froben became Erasmus' printer-in-chief; being indeed far above any possibility of competition. Not that he absorbed everything which Erasmus produced; for others had claims in the name of friendship which could not be overlooked. Schurer wrote asking for something to print,[5] and received Quintus Curtius, a substantial folio:[6] besides reprinting other works which had issued first elsewhere. During Erasmus' residence in the Netherlands, too, it was naturally more convenient for him to print with Martens, who was on the spot. Accordingly at Louvain appeared a great number of small volumes—the first two collections of Erasmus' Letters, some of his Apologies, and most of his Paraphrases on the Epistles of the New Testament: both the latter series beginning in 1517. One point of interest about the Paraphrases is the extreme rarity of some of Martens' editions: Romans is fairly common, but of Corinthians I know of

---

[1] *Ep.* 332, 6–9.   [2] 6 February 1515.
[3] *Epp.* 328, 36–7; 330, 1.   [4] *Epp.* 348, 10–12; 356, 11–12.
[5] *Epp.* 606; 612, 33–5; 633.   [6] *Epp.* 693; 704.

only three copies, of Galatians two, of Peter two, of
Hebrews one, of James only a trace in a catalogue which
cannot be verified: and from this scanty list one would
have to be deducted all round, if the Bibliothèque Nation-
ale had not recently acquired a composite volume containing the first five paraphrases mentioned. The editions
were no doubt small, for a reason which I shall presently
suggest.

The earlier Apologies were printed by Martens: but
when his antagonists were connected closely with Louvain, Erasmus judged it wiser to have the books produced elsewhere, so that there might be no fear of the
contents leaking out before the whole was ready for
publication. Thus the Apology against Latomus was
given to John Theobald at Antwerp, the three replies to
Lee to Michael Hillen: who also was the first to print one
of the Paraphrases, on Timothy, Titus, and Philemon,
in 1519, and a new edition of the *Ratio verae Theologiae*
in 1523; the latter volume being so rare that, in spite
of frequent enquiries, I cannot find a single copy of it,
though of its existence there can be no doubt since
Erasmus mentions it specifically in the Catalogue of his
writings[1] which he drew up in 1524.

But these exceptions were few. So long as Froben
lived he could command practically everything that he
wished of Erasmus' output, especially the big volumes.
All the editions of the Fathers, Cyprian, Arnobius,
Hilary, Jerome (the second edition), Irenaeus, Athanasius, Ambrose, Augustine; the Paraphrases on the
Gospels and Acts, which first came to the light in handsome folio, instead of Martens' quartos; the big volumes
of letters, and hosts of smaller works—all of these bear
Froben's mark, the serpents twining round a staff on

[1] *Cat. Lucub.*, p. 40, 29–30.

which stands a dove, and give evidence of his constant improvement in technique. Between the brilliant author and the sturdy printer the atmosphere was not always unclouded. 'I should wonder at nothing in Froben: I know him too well. But I am surprised that Lachner does not take you into counsel:' so Erasmus complains[1] to Beatus Rhenanus in 1517. 'Froben doesn't see how much labour goes into a book:[2] he merely counts the pages he has to set up.' 'Froben seems to prefer to be served by fools.'[3] Between friends working together but separated by distance and often not meeting for years, occasional grumblings need not surprise us. They are in marked contrast to the continual efforts[4] made by Froben to persuade Erasmus to return to Basle; and to the heartfelt grief with which Erasmus deplored his friend's death in October 1527.

This event produced considerable derangement in the affairs of the firm. Jerome, the eldest son, was twenty-six, and had already taken some part in the business; but John Erasmius was not yet twelve. In consequence his mother, Gertrude Lachner, Froben's second wife, set about finding a partner. With more decision than judgement she selected John Herwagen, who for five years had been printing in Strasburg; and with the connubial facility of the age quickly set seal to the bargain by marrying him. Through 1528 the firm appears as Herwagen and Froben, in 1529 it became Froben and Herwagen, and in September it was strengthened by the addition of Nicholas Episcopius, who had married Justina Froben, sister of John Erasmius. This combination lasted till March 1531; but later Herwagen went out. He was an unsatisfactory character, who brought discord into the family; and ten

---

[1] *Ep.* 628, 1, 2.
[2] *Epp.* 629, 7–9; 733, 6–8.
[3] *Ep.* 705, 5–6.
[4] *Epp.* 582, 14–18; 801–2.

years afterwards he brought himself to complete disrepute
by seducing the young wife of his stepson, John Erasmius,
with whom he had been in partnership since 1538.

Through these vicissitudes Erasmus remained faithful
to the firm; and even after the split in 1531 he continued
to have dealings with Herwagen—no doubt for Gertrude
Lachner's sake, with whom he had ties extending back
over many years.[1] The *Epistolae Floridae* appeared in
September 1531, under Herwagen's mark, a triple Hermes
holding in his hand a staff round which the prudent serpents twined, but lacking—a significant omission—the
harmless dove. Next year he wrote a preface[2] for Herwagen's Demosthenes in the Greek, as he had written[3]
for Bebel's Greek Aristotle in 1531. But it was not work
he liked, and he declined to go on, his refusal being perhaps connected with dislike for Herwagen.[4] Meanwhile,
during the months that followed Froben's death, he had
taken up with John Faber Emmeus of Juliers, who had
been printing in Basle since 1526. He wrote a preface for
a small treatise by Faustus, Bishop of Reggio, which
Emmeus printed in 1528; and when the printer, like
himself, took refuge at Freiburg in 1529, to escape the
religious innovations at Basle, a new tie was created
between them. Emmeus received a number of small
books, including treatises of Alger and Basil, edited by
Erasmus; but the most considerable volumes that he
produced for the *réfugié* scholar were the important
Epistolae Palaeonaeoi, September 1532—now very rare—
and the works of Haymo, 1533, both in folio.

The loss of Froben brought another publisher into
Erasmus' view, Claude Chevallon, for whom Badius had

---

[1] *Ep.* 419, 18 n., 19 n.   [2] Lond., xxviii, 26; LB., 1228.
[3] Lond., xxviii, 13; LB., 1159.
[4] *Epp. Fam. Erasmi ad Bonif. Amerbachium*, 1779, nos. 73, 92, 78.

printed occasionally since 1506. As soon as the news
reached Paris, Chevallon wrote to Erasmus to propose
an edition of Augustine. It was doubtless well-known
throughout the world of letters that for years Froben
had been preparing for a new edition which should be an
improvement on John Amorbach's of 1506, and that
Erasmus was in charge; and Chevallon would have been
glad to carry on the project if he could secure it. But
Erasmus replied that a beginning had already been made
with the printing—indeed the preface to vol. ii is dated
in October 1527, the month of Froben's death. Nothing
daunted, however, Chevallon turned off to Ambrose, of
whom Froben had printed an edition by Erasmus in
August 1527. With the help of a few manuscripts
gathered from different sources, one of which was the rich
library of the Abbey of St. Victor, he was able to claim
some novelty for the edition; but in the main his four
volumes, completed in February 1529, are a reprint of
Froben's. Later in the year the Basle Augustine appeared. Chevallon had it examined by a German scholar,
James Haemer of Stuttgart; who formed the conclusion
that Erasmus' work had been hurriedly done without
sufficient reference to authorities. So again manuscripts
were borrowed from St. Victor's, and Haemer revised
the text anew, pointing out also a number of Erasmus'
errors. This edition appeared in 1531, and in the next
year Chevallon reprinted a volume of translations from
Gregory Nazianzen made by Pirckheimer, which Erasmus
had edited for Froben and Episcopius in September 1531,
after Pirckheimer's death. First a new issue, with a few
additions; then a critical revision; and finally an un-
blushing reprint. Such action must surely have seemed
unfriendly. Yet in two years' time we find a complete edition of Jerome published by Chevallon; again Erasmus'

text revised with manuscripts from St. Victor's, but this time with his co-operation—correction of his scholia and a new preface added. This was followed in 1536 by Chrysostom in five volumes, based on the edition published by the Frobens for Erasmus in 1530; but rearranged and with some new material incorporated—translations made by Erasmus and Germanus Brixius of Auxerre, and printed by the Frobens in 1533. In this too Erasmus' co-operation is shown by the inclusion of his translation of Chrysostom's *Missa*, made twenty-five years before for John Fisher, but never yet printed.[1] The preface to the whole edition by Chevallon's corrector, John Hucherius of Verneuil, is dated 1 July 1536, within a few days of Erasmus' death.

But again these are the exceptions. Apart from them almost everything that Erasmus produced during his last years went to Froben and Episcopius, books great and small. In June 1535, he was at length ready to print a work on preaching, *Ecclesiastes*, which he had long had in hand. He returned to Basle, to Jerome Froben's hospitable house 'Zum Luft' in the Bäumleingasse; and by August the book was published. This was to have marked the term of his visit, but he found it hard to leave friends and scenes so long beloved. Lingering on and on he at length let himself be persuaded to have his effects brought over from Freiburg. One motive which impelled him to stay was an edition of Origen, which with his ceaseless activity he had undertaken as soon as the *Ecclesiastes* was finished. But he was not to see the end. It appeared in September, but by that time 'the Master' had been two months dead, leaving as his heir Boniface Amerbach, and as his executors his two publisher-friends, Froben and Episcopius.

[1] *Ep.* 227, 1 n.

As early as 1524 Erasmus had contemplated a collected
edition of his writings, in nine or ten volumes.[1] By a will
of 22 January 1527 he gave directions how this should
be done. Froben, who was then living, was to undertake
it if he would, and to receive 1,200 florins, spread over
three or four years. Some correctors were to be engaged,
at salaries varying from 40 to 100 florins a year: and their
instructions were to correct printers' errors, or evident
mistakes of the author, after careful consideration. But
on no account were they to interpolate additions of their
own—a provision which illustrates the editorial practice
of the time. A further injunction was, to be extremely
careful in reproducing quotations from other authors.
Fifteen hundred copies were to be printed, at the least,
and of these twenty were to be well bound, for special
presentation. The first six recipients enumerated were
English; Warham, Tunstall, More, Longlond, Fisher, and
the library of Queens' College, Cambridge. By his will of
12 February 1536 these provisions were confirmed, under
a clause which renewed everything in the earlier document which was not specifically changed. The edition
was undertaken at once by Jerome Froben and Episcopius[2] and completed in 1540; having been supervised
by Beatus Rhenanus, who dedicated it to the Emperor
with a preface which was a life of Erasmus. The special
copies were no doubt distributed, as Erasmus directed;
but I have not yet succeeded in tracing any one of them.

In conclusion, a few points of general interest arise.
On the question of copyright I have not read enough to
justify me in handling so wide a subject. But it may
perhaps be worth while to give some illustrations of
current practice from Erasmus' letters down to 1519.
One need only turn over the pages of that immense under-

[1] *Cat. Lucub.*, pp. 38–42.   [2] Beatus Rhenanus, *Ep.* 300.

taking, the Ghent bibliography of Erasmus, to realize that his works were constantly reprinted, during his lifetime as well as after his death, by printers whom he never knew: Froben's title-pages being imitated to the extent even of reproducing such warranties as 'nunc primum natum et aeditum' or 'denuo ab autore recognitum'. Many of these reprints appeared within a few months of the original issue; and were presumably pirated, not a penny of profit returning to either Erasmus or his authorized printer. Even reputable firms reproduced one another's books. Froben, as we have seen, reprinted in 1513 the Aldine edition of Erasmus' *Adagia*, 1508; and in return the Asulani in September 1520 reprinted the Froben edition of 1517–18. But there is nothing to show that any consideration passed between the firms, for permission. Another instance, revealed by an autograph letter of Erasmus to Froben,[1] is amusing for the misconception which it creates at first sight. The letter begins: 'Badius has imitated your book, but has put in a preface in which he says that he is selling it at half the price of the original. You had better add something like this'; after which comes a preface in Froben's name addressed to the reader and complaining of printers who try to undersell honest work. I found myself quite unable to identify the book mentioned, but M. Philippe Renouard with his unrivalled knowledge of Badius' work gave me the clue by return of post, referring me to Froben's edition of the *Antiquae Lectiones* of Caelius Rhodiginus, on the title-page of which stands the preface composed by Erasmus. Further investigation showed that Badius produced the same book a few months earlier than Froben, and that the book in question was an Aldine publication which they were both reprinting, no doubt

[1] *Ep.* 602.

without licence. Thus the meaning of Erasmus' opening
sentences was to warn Froben, not of Badius' piracy
against him, but of their competition in piracy against
another.

Copyright was a point on which Badius was sensitive.
In 1512, when Erasmus sent him a number of books to
print, he replied:[1] 'Don't think me ungrateful for not
making a better offer; but there is such competition,
printers waiting with their presses ready for anything
that comes out from me, that I really cannot afford more.
These books that you send, too, will only give them
justification; for the *Enchiridion* will offend Martens, the
Moria Gourmont and the *De ratione studii* de Keysere,
who printed them before.' As stated above, Badius had
received the first edition of the *De Copia*; but when a
new edition was produced by Schurer in December 1514
with a new preface by Erasmus, he considered that he had
some ground of complaint. He writes loyally, however,
to his friend[2] in August 1515: 'About your volume of
Adagia (perhaps the transaction of two years before)
Berckman has dealt honestly with me; but the new
German edition (of the *De Copia*) will injure the sale of
mine. Still, if it is to your profit, I will not complain.'
Again in 1516 he for a time declined to reprint the
Parabolae, as Erasmus had invited him, on the ground
that Martens had recently reprinted it: though, mindful
of the injury about the *De Copia*, he was not prepared to
trouble about the interests of Schurer, who had printed
the first edition.[3] Later he explained the situation to
Erasmus,[4] without ambiguity:

'I am complimented by your proposal, but I don't wish to
cause to others the loss they cause to me. Let me make this

[1] *Ep.* 263, 5–10.   [2] *Ep.* 346, 5–8; cf. *Ep.* 434, 5–8.
[3] *Ep.* 434, 1–8.   [4] *Ep.* 472, 1–14.

clear. Your fame is now so great that when a new edition of any of your works comes out, with indication of revision, although there may be nothing new added, people will not touch the earlier issues. In this way I have suffered great losses in the *De Copia*, the Panegyric and the *Moria*; also in the *Enchiridion*, of which I bought 500 copies, and the *Adagia* of which I took 110. It would be more to our profit if you would give one work to one printer, and make no change till he had sold his edition right out: as you seem to have done to some extent with the *Parabolae*, if you gave Schurer a warning (?not to print too many), and if Martens reprinted it without encouragement from you. In the Panegyric too I was greatly disappointed; for at your suggestion I sent a good number of copies to Germany, and then found they had been printed there (by Froben in April, 1516).'

Nevertheless, in spite of these words, Badius reprinted the *Parabolae* in November.

His protests had some effect. In the spring of 1517 Erasmus complained to Froben that Martens had been damaged by Froben's action in reprinting the first volume of Gaza's Grammar. Beatus Rhenanus' reply[1] indicates the difficulties that surrounded the position. 'A printer from Louvain brought it here to sell for the best price he could get; and if Froben hadn't bought it from him, for a volume of the New Testament, somebody else would have, for there were many eager to obtain it.' But later on, though appearing to disapprove of such reprinting, Erasmus is encouraging it again. In November 1517 Martens had printed the first of Erasmus' Paraphrases, on the Epistle to the Romans.[2] In December, Erasmus writes thus to Beatus from Louvain:[3]

'I was going to send the Paraphrase to Basle, as it is the sort of thing to sell well; but as Froben seemed to have enough on hand, I gave it to the good Martens. I send you now a copy of his edition corrected: but it would perhaps be better not to

---

[1] *Ep.* 575, 1–5. [2] *Ep.* 710. [3] *Ep.* 732, 15–24.

reprint our poor friend's book at once. He has never reprinted anything of Froben's except the *Institutio Principis*, which he did without my knowledge when I was away in England: and I scolded him well for it. I do my best to prevent his injuring you.'

These assurances were repeated at the same time to Lachner.[1] But the value of them is shown by the fact that Froben's edition of the Paraphrase appeared next month!

So it was indeed with almost every one of Erasmus' works. Froben's issues followed Martens' almost as soon as they could be carried to Basle and set up; Schurer's followed Froben's: so, too, the printers of Cologne and Paris and Antwerp. Erasmus connived at this, for many of the new issues bear evidences of his revision, as Badius complained. The inference seems to be that though the printers deprecated imitation of their own works, and fully realized that it was unfriendly to imitate the works of others, still the situation as regards the enforcement of any protection of copyright was hopeless. They knew that they were doing one another wrong. But business was business, and in the pursuit of present gain they were not ashamed to go on still in their wickedness. Seemingly all that they could do to protect themselves was not to print too large an edition: and that is perhaps why some of Martens' volumes are so rare.

[1] *Ep.* 733, 12–14.

THE TRILINGUAL COLLEGES OF THE EARLY SIXTEENTH CENTURY

THE *necessitas* of the early sixteenth century was not *trinoda* but *trilinguis*: the three languages being those necessary for the study of the Bible, the languages which Jerome had rejoiced to know, Hebrew and Greek and Latin. The word had now gone forth that for the serious student translations were inadequate: and that he could not be content, henceforward, with anything less than the original text of his author in the language in which it had been written. Aldus at Venice had affirmed this principle in the schools of the philosophers by producing his great edition of Aristotle in the Greek, 1495–9; and two years later, in 1501, he appealed to the theologians by announcing—what he never in fact undertook—an edition of the Bible in the three languages. The new conception did not, of course, go unchallenged. The great conservative party, stolid, obstructive, for ever dying in the last ditch—those tenacious allies, to whom all who love the past are so profoundly indebted—arose in its might, and with arguments indifferent and bad proceeded once more to oppose in vain.

Hebrew was the language of the Jews, a race then so despised that even the most fair-minded of contemporary thinkers could find little to say on their behalf. Greek was the language of a heretical church; and there was no reason to suppose that Greek manuscripts were more correct than Latin—indeed it was possible that on behalf of their special doctrines the Greeks might prove to have corrupted their manuscripts intentionally. But above all, to find fault with the Vulgate was to impugn the great name of Jerome, whose version of the Scriptures the Church had contentedly read for centuries, and in reliance on whom countless scholars of renown had been satisfied to know no Greek.

Ditches, first or last, are poor things with which to meet the rising tide. The new principle was too evident, too reasonable, for the issue to be for a moment in doubt. Before the century was many years old, colleges appropriated to the study of the three languages began to rise in all parts of Europe. First of these may be mentioned the college aptly named after St. Jerome in Ximenes' splendid university at Alcalá; though it was a part of his plan which did not actually come into being till 1528. At Cambridge the Lady Margaret, under the guidance of Bishop Fisher, founded first Christ's and then St. John's, to be the houses of the new studies. To the University of Rome, 'Sapientia' as it was called, Leo X presented a College of Greek, with John Lascaris at its head. In Oxford Fox with Corpus Christi and Wolsey with Cardinal College helped the movement forward. In Paris Francis I made the first beginnings of the famous Collège de France. Jerome Busleiden planted a college of the three languages in the centre of the highly orthodox University of Louvain. So too with the University of Wittenberg, soon to be the home of Luther and of all that was unorthodox, the intention of its founder, Duke Frederic of Saxony, was that it should be definitely trilingual. At Mainz Ulrich von Hutten tried to persuade his patron, the youthful Archbishop-Elector, to found a college on the same lines. At Vienna menaced by the Turks, the stoutly Catholic bishop Faber created the trilingual college of St. Nicholas; and at Leipzig, Heidelberg, and Ingolstadt the movement found favour with the ducal patrons of those universities. In the compass of a single paper it is not possible to examine in detail these numerous institutions. Instead of passing them all briefly in review, it seems better to select three, which present interesting differences in form, and examine them at some length: bearing in mind that whatever the diversities of outward appearance, arising out of differences of local conditions, the intention underlying them all was the same—the recovery of languages then really dead, languages in which were enshrined the most precious treasures of human thought and expression.

To begin with the University of Alcalá, founded about 1500—the date is not quite certain—its builder, Fray Francisco Ximenes de Cisneros, was then at the height of his power. His had been an eventful life. Six of his best years, thirty-seven to forty-three, had been spent in prison, for disputing with a superior over a benefice to which the Pope had presented him. After long austerities as an Observant, the strictest sect of the Franciscans, he had returned to the world, master of himself and fitted to become a master of others. He had attracted the notice of the Grand Cardinal Mendoza, Archbishop of Toledo, who in 1492 moved Isabella to choose him as her confessor, and on his death-bed urged the Queen to nominate him as his successor in the see of Toledo. Isabella assented, and thus in 1495 Ximenes reluctantly found himself, when within a year of sixty, Primate of Spain and master of enormous revenues.

Though no scholar himself, he was keenly alive to the importance of those two main products of a university, education and learning; and set himself to apply his great wealth to the promotion of them. His first idea was to found a college to be the home in Spain of the Scotist philosophy: which as yet had received little attention there. But as he revolved this scheme in his mind, it expanded rapidly. He was dissatisfied with the possibilities offered by the existing Castilian universities, Salamanca was too conservative, Siguenza was scarcely beginning, Valladolid—where his predecessor Mendoza had founded the fine college of Santa Cruz, to match San Gregorio, the creation of a Bishop of Burgos—was too frequently the residence of the court to offer the quiet and retirement desirable for study and research. So he chose as the site of his new foundation the ancient Roman city of Complutum, named by the Moors Alcalá, the castle, beside the quiet waters of the Henares. It was a town of some importance in those days, before Madrid had out-rivalled it. There was a royal palace in which our Queen Catherine of Aragon was born in 1485, and Ferdinand the Emperor in 1503. Later, Alcalá was the birthplace of Cervantes, 1547, and in its town school Ximenes himself had begun his education in the middle of the fifteenth century. It lies in a broad, pleasant valley, with green hills to the south near by; and northwards the ground rises slowly to a low ridge, beyond which shine the summits of the Guadarrama, snow-covered even in May.

By 1500 Ximenes had resolved what he would do. He would build there a complete university, which should embrace the whole circle of learning, ancient and modern. Whenever he could snatch a few days' leisure from his duties as Primate, he used to make his way to Alcalá and watch the rising walls. By 1508 ten colleges were in being, forty-two professors installed in their chairs; and the first students were admitted, with an opening ceremony to which Ximenes invited distinguished scholars from Salamanca and from Paris. About the same time he persuaded the well-known printer, Arnold of Brocario, to leave Pamplona and assume the charge of the University Press. To set a definite character upon his new institution he allotted to it the task which Aldus had not carried out—to print the Bible complete in its original languages. The story of his great undertaking has been veiled beneath the modesty of its editors. Except in one volume, the New Testament, where one of the final leaves has a few verses in praise of the book and of Ximenes, there is nothing to show who did the work of collating and editing and translating. The names above the verses are those of Demetrios Doukas of Crete, Nicetas Faustus, Fernando Nuñez of Valladolid, Bartolomeo de Castro of Burgos, and the youthful Juan Vergara of Toledo: to whom Vives in his notes on Augustine, *De Civitate Dei*, 1522, ascribes a prominent part in the Greek. Besides these Alfonso of Zamora made some of the translations from the Hebrew; and two other famous scholars are mentioned as having assisted in the work, Diego Lopez Zuniga (Stunica), who was afterwards a severe critic of Erasmus' orthodoxy, and the famous Antonio of Lebrija (Nebrissensis), who about the end of 1514 was driven out of Salamanca by the conservative party, and found a warm welcome awaiting him at Alcalá.

From the preface written in Ximenes' name to dedicate the book to Leo X it appears that the manuscripts for the Hebrew and Aramaic of the Old Testament were collected from Spain: where after, or perhaps in consequence of, the recent expulsion of the Jews (1492), they were plentiful. For seven Hebrew manuscripts alone 4,000 crowns are said to have been given. Besides these the senate of Venice sent a Greek manuscript of the greater part of the Old Testament copied specially for Ximenes from an early manuscript which had belonged to Bessarion; and Leo X on the 27th of August 1513, within a few months of his accession to the Papacy, instructed his librarian to issue a Greek manuscript, also

of the greater part of the Old Testament, to Alfonso
Garcia del Rincon, Abbot of Alcalá, after receiving a
suitable deposit in the name of Ximenes—adding that
even if the manuscript should happen to be chained or
otherwise confined to the library, that should be no
obstacle. The researches of Delitzsch have led to the
discovery of this manuscript in the Vatican; two volumes
written in the fourteenth century, and now numbered
346 and 330. The preface to the New Testament mentions that Leo lent manuscripts for that also; but these
have not been identified. From Rhodes, then within a
few years of falling to the Turks, came a manuscript of
the Epistles sent as an offering to Ximenes, perhaps by
Spanish knights wishing to pay their homage to the
conqueror of Oran (1509); but of this too no trace can
now be found. For the Vulgate a great number of Latin
manuscripts were examined; the most ancient being one
in the Alcalá University Library, written in 'Gothic'
character and said to be 800 years old.

The work of preparation is said to have begun in 1502:
it no doubt occupied many years. On the 10th of January
1514—less than five months after the loan of the Vatican
manuscript—Brocario put the colophon to the first
volume completed, the New Testament; in 1515 the
second volume, containing a Hebrew and Aramaic lexicon
with other aids to the student, was ready; on the 10th of
July 1517 the four volumes of the Old Testament were
finished for Ximenes' inspection. The whole cost of the
edition was estimated at 50,000 crowns. Thereafter the
book has a curious history. Ximenes died in November
1517 without having decided, or obtained leave, to publish it: and so the sheets of the six volumes, printed off
but unbound, remained in Brocario's warehouse, until on
the 22nd of March 1520 the Pope issued a licence to the

executors to put the book into circulation. Thus it came
about that before the New Testament made its appearance, in spite of its prior date, it had been twice antici-
pated; by Erasmus' edition, Basle 1516, and by the
Aldine Greek Bible, 1518. The delay was no doubt due
in part to the death of the Cardinal of Spain; but another
cause may be found in Leo's unwillingness to sanction
publication until the manuscripts had returned in safety
to the Vatican. On the 7th of January 1519 his patience
was exhausted. They had been borrowed for a year,
with a pledge of 200 ducats sustained by the Archbishop
of Bari; and they had been retained for more than five.
So Leo wrote to the Archbishop of Cosenza, then nuncio
in Spain, asking him to negotiate for their return; and
on the 9th of July 1519 they were once more in the
Vatican. The papal permission to publish followed in
due course; but even so publication was slow, and it
was not till 1522 that copies reached Erasmus at Basle
and Vives in Louvain. Leo's care for his manuscripts was
in advance of the practice of the time; to judge from
the cautions Erasmus thought it well to inscribe in two
manuscripts he was returning to the Austin priory of
Corsendonk, on the 19th of May 1519: *seruetur* in one,
φυλαχθήτω in the other. The manuscript sent to Ximenes from Venice is still preserved in the 'Fondo Com-
plutense' of the University Library of Madrid: whither
the treasures of Alcalá were transferred with the University in 1836.

The assertion of the inadequacy of translations and
of the importance of studying originals, put into the
'Cardinal of Spain's' mouth in his preface to Leo X,
is worth quoting:

'Every language has its own characteristics of style, the full
force of which cannot be reproduced by any translation, how-

ever accurate: and this is especially true in the language through which the mouth of the Lord has spoken. For though the letter of this is dead and like the flesh which profiteth nothing (for it is the Spirit that quickeneth), nevertheless because Christ veiled in forms of words remains pent within its womb, clearly it must be so full of amazing richness, so piled up with inexhaustible store of mysteries, that since it is always brimming and running over, out of its body must flow rivers of living water. From these streams those to whom it is given to behold the glory of the Lord unveiled, that they may be transformed into the same likeness, may drink in without ceasing the wonderful secrets of that Godhead: since from every word, from every combination of letters, well up and burst forth the most hidden senses of heavenly wisdom. And since even the most learned translator cannot express more than one of these, it follows that after translation the Scripture still remains pregnant with many sublime meanings, which cannot be known except by drinking at the fountain of the original language.'

But that Ximenes' outlook was not entirely theological is shown by another great project that he embraced, before the Bible was completed—a new edition of Aristotle in the Greek, with a new translation side by side; but before more than a small part of the new translation had been made (by Vergara), he was dead. The splendid University he had founded lived on as the centre of humanism in Spain, and a brilliant rival to Salamanca. Its freedom from old-fashioned restraints is shown by the fact that in the next generation one of the chairs of rhetoric was filled by a daughter of Antonio of Lebrija, with great success.

For the Oxford foundations of the same period the credit must be shared between Fox and Wolsey; who co-operated in a scheme to encourage the new studies. The former designed to add a college to the University, and according to a tradition had intended that it should be a monastic foundation appropriated to young monks from St. Swithin's at Winchester, on the same footing as Gloucester Hall or St. Mary's College: till Oldham, bishop of Exeter, who contributed to the funds of the new institution, persuaded him to abandon the 'buzzing monks' and consecrate it to the new aims of learning. The building began in 1515, and on the 20th of June 1517 Fox, sitting in the great church of his predecessor, Henry of Blois, at St. Cross, by Winchester, gave his Statutes for the College of Corpus Christi. The principal feature of the college was the establishment of three public Readers: right skilful herbalists to plant herbs and flowers for his ingenious bees—a pleasant simile to which Fox recurs again and again in his Statutes. The Reader of the Arts of Humanity was to plant the Latin tongue, and 'manfully to root out barbarity from our garden should it at any time germinate therein'. The Reader of the Grecists—appointed in compliance with the mandate of the Council of Vienne, 1311—was publicly to read and clearly to explain Greek on common or half-holidays; and 'the third gardener, whom it behoves the other gardeners to obey, wait on, and serve' was the reader in Sacred Divinity.

Just about the same time the attention of Wolsey also was directed to Oxford. Opposition to the nascent study of Greek had led to unseemly disturbances; and it seemed desirable for external influence to do something for the reform of the studies of the University. In the summer of 1518 the 'Cardinal of England' announced that he would institute six public readerships, humanity, rhetoric, theology, and canon law being among the subjects chosen; and at the same time, with the consent of the Chancellor, Archbishop Warham, he undertook, at the University's request, to revise its Statutes. These projects led him on to the foundation of Cardinal College, in which his public Readers should dwell. But until their house was ready for them, he arranged with Fox to lodge them near by, in Corpus Christi. In consequence it is not easy to determine the precise scope of Fox's designs. Though his third Reader was to be occupied with sacred Divinity, and receive the 'services of the other two 'gardeners', it is noticeable that there is no mention of Hebrew among the subjects to which he was to pay attention; and that this omission was not fortuitous may be argued from the composition of the library which Fox presented to Corpus. As a nucleus for it he acquired an interesting collection of books which had been bought at Rome in the earliest days of printing by his predecessor in the see of Durham, John Shirwood († 1493): three dozen of the Latin classics and Latin Fathers. To these he added a Bible; Vincent of Beauvais, to be their encyclopaedia; a few books on law and medicine; some of the Schoolmen and the moderns; numerous Latin classics, and finally a full set of the Aldine Greek classics—a magnificent equipment for a library which was to be up to date. Yet Erasmus wrote to Claymond, Fox's first President, in 1519 of *trilinguis ista biblio-theca*; Fisher in 1526 praises to Fox this college of theologians, with its special teachers of Hebrew, Greek, and Latin. Of this apparent contradiction two explanations are possible: firstly there was a scarcity of Hebrew books and teachers, of which there is more to be said hereafter; secondly Wolsey, whose Readers at first filled the place of Fox's, may have allocated one of his posts to Hebrew, and so have made it unnecessary for Fox to do the same. Certainly Oxford's first Hebraist at this period, Robert Wakefeld, was attached to Henry VIII's foundation which arose out of Cardinal College.

Though Fox had constructed his 'apiary' either wholly or chiefly for the sake of Sacred Divinity, in charge of the third and chief gardener, he did not lose sight of the classics—the *melior eruditio* or *politior literatura* or *literae amoeniores*, which men were then preferring, with expressive comparison, above the 'barbarous' studies of the philosophers and the lawyers; who were so occupied with the matter of their discourse as to pay no heed to its form. His books, as we have seen, included practically all of the classics, both Greek and Latin, then available; and his statutes direct his Readers to the most notable authors, classical and modern. The Reader of the Arts of Humanity had prescribed for him on different days of the week Cicero and Quintilian and Pliny, Sallust and Suetonius and Valerius Maximus; Terence and Plautus, Virgil and Ovid and Lucan, Horace and Juvenal and Persius; and then, classed together, Laurentius Valla, Aulus Gellius, and Politian. The Greek Reader might make his choice from Homer and Hesiod and Pindar, Sophocles and Euripides and Aristophanes, Thucydides and Theophrastus and Plutarch, Plato and Aristotle, Isocrates, Theocritus, Lucian, Philostratus; and for grammar was prescribed Theodore Gaza. Fox's Statutes are so long—Ward's translation of them occupies 235 octavo pages—that it seems doubtful whether they can have been his handiwork, except in outline. Then, as now, a Bishop of Winchester had little leisure; and in 1517 Fox had just retired from important office in the government, worn out with its cares and nearing seventy. It would have been natural for him to commit the details, at least of educational matters, and the Latin composition to some competent and younger hand. A person whose name suggests itself is John Stokesley, a fellow of Magdalen College, Oxford, who had just returned from

Italy *trium linguarum gnarus* or endowed with *triplex lingua*. He was for a time Fox's chaplain, and was present at St. Cross when Fox gave his Statutes—the only man of letters specified in the whole company; subsequently he rose to distinction as Dean of the Chapel Royal and Bishop of London.

One noticeable feature of Fox's or Wolsey's appointments—in the early years it is not possible to distinguish them and such records as there are do not separate the Greek from the Latin Readers—is that the first holders of these chairs were young and untried men. John Clement, when he was appointed in 1518, can scarcely have been more than twenty-three; and though both More and Linacre thought highly of his attainments, he had no publications to his name to support his selection. He had taught More's children, and helped Colet to make a beginning with Greek, but fame did not come to him till after he had left Oxford and made his way to Italy to study medicine, in which his interests really lay. As he passed from More's household to Wolsey's a few months before his appointment to Oxford, it seems likely that he was Wolsey's choice rather than Fox's. So too with Clement's successor in 1519–20, Thomas Lupset. He was only about twenty-one, and had done nothing more than to see through the press—as proof-reader, not editor—a translation from Galen by Linacre and the second edition of More's *Utopia*, both printed in Paris in 1517. He had been a favourite with Colet, who had sent him as one of the earliest scholars to the renovated St. Paul's school in 1511; he had helped Erasmus in collating the New Testament at Cambridge in 1513; and he had been in Italy with Pace. But that was all. Except for the favour of his friends he had as yet no claim to distinction. In his case, too, the appointment came from Wolsey: whom the University wrote to thank, giving an account of his lectures. But the unproductiveness of these first Readers was soon to be removed, after they left Oxford. The final preface to the Aldine *editio princeps* of Galen, which appeared in five folio volumes in 1525, mentions four Englishmen and one German as having laboured with the correction of the text: the former were Clement and Lupset; a certain Odoardus who was perhaps David Edwards, Scholar of Corpus in 1517, aged fifteen; and one Roseus, whom I am unable to identify.

When Lupset left Oxford in 1523, Wolsey appointed in his place the Spaniard, Vives: a somewhat older man, thirty-one, but not yet of the distinction that he reached later. His life had been spent mostly at Paris and Louvain, and he had been tutor to Ximenes' successor, the young Fleming, William of Croy, who in defiance of Spanish feeling had been permitted to acquire preferment and draw great revenues from the Peninsula he never visited. Vives came to England in the autumn of 1522, bringing with him the only considerable book he had yet published—a fine edition of Augustine's *De Civitate Dei*, dedicated to Henry VIII; but this visit, like an earlier one in 1517, failed to procure him employment. Next year, however, he tried his fortune again, this time having in his pocket an invitation from Alcalá to succeed Antonio of Lebrija, who had died in the summer of 1522. The proof that the prophet was not without honour even in his own country perhaps made the difference. Wolsey accepted him and sent him to Oxford: where he taught at intervals for some years, and according to a legend attracted a swarm of real bees, who were still making honey in the leads above his room at Corpus, one hundred years after he had left Oxford for good.

Of the books actually taught by these early Readers, as compared with those enjoined in Fox's Statutes, there is not much indication. Lupset lectured on Proclus' *Sphere*, a mathematical work which Linacre had translated for Aldus in 1499. Vives at the end of his first session reported to Wolsey that he had begun to eject Albertus Magnus from the schools, and that in dialectic and other fields of philosophy he had removed many *prauae opiniones*. The strongly humanistic character of his teaching may also be seen in the courses he prescribed for the reading of boys and girls: though he mingles with the classics a number of Christian poets whose names are now unfamiliar. That Sacred Divinity was not neglected by Fox's third gardener may be inferred from some Latin translations of Chrysostom (in manuscript in the Bodleian), made by John Helyar, a young scholar of Corpus and pupil of Vives: presumably from a volume of the Greek dedicated by Erasmus to Claymond, the first President, in 1526. Wood credits him also with scholia on Sophocles and commentaries on Cicero and Ovid.

Some idea of Oxford studies in the year 1520, just when Wolsey's Readers were getting to work may be gathered from a unique document which has chanced to be preserved in the Corpus Library; the 'day book' of one John Dorne or Thorne, a Brunswicker who after failure as a printer had settled in Oxford as a bookseller, and was accustomed to replenish his stock by periodical visits to the book fairs of the Continent. The day-book has been edited and elucidated by Mr. Falconer Madan for the Oxford Historical Society; and Mr. Salter has discovered the actual position of Dorne's shop, on a site in the High opposite St. Mary's, next but one to Grove Street—precisely where thirty years ago there was still a bookshop. Dorne's lists of daily sales show that his wares were for all kinds of customers: theologians and lawyers; students of medicine and classics; clergy who bought mass books; schoolboys who wanted the grammars of Stanbridge and Whittinton and little books of colloquial Latin, and finally the general public who came to him for almanacks, ballads and Christmas carols. The classical books are in fair proportion, but usually the sale is quite occasional, a Virgil or Cicero or Ovid or Terence at intervals: no great demand, for Theology and the other superior faculties still dominated the schools, and Arts was enthralled by philosophy. But in August 1520 on returning from the Continent Dorne had brought with him copies of the *Plutus* of Aristophanes—a favourite with the Renaissance, and recently published in the Greek by Martens at Louvain in a form convenient for the needy student. Within a week he had sold eleven copies—a fact which suggests that Clement had found out the opportunity offered, and had at once formed a class to read Greek.

The reasons for the appointment of untried men to these Oxford readerships are not far to seek. In Italy competent teachers might have been found with ease. Spain, which was in direct communication with Italian learning through the Spanish College at Bologna, could produce the New Testament in Greek—an undertaking which would have been quite impossible at the same date in England. But in the north things were far different. In a generation earlier the only Greek available to teach such men as Reuchlin, Budaeus, Erasmus, Beatus Rhenanus, was the incompetent George Hermonymus of Sparta; and now things were little better, at any rate in England. The older men such as Grocin and Linacre, who had at one time lectured on Greek, were past such work: Latimer had long abandoned those studies; Colet and Fisher, even if they had known Greek, were too much occupied with their official duties; Tunstall and More and Pace had gone off into the excitements offered by the service of the Crown. The position at Oxford may be judged from a letter of Linacre to Claymond, Fox's first President of Corpus, urging him, in the earlier period, when he was President of Magdalen, to learn Greek. Linacre's letter runs as follows:

'London. I am sending back to you the boy who is our joint-pupil: not much more learned than when he came, but perhaps with a little more chance of becoming learned some day. I have given him some light upon grammar and rhetoric: which may save him from wandering from the right path, and help him to keep his eyes open as he goes along. Upon these arts I laid the utmost stress from the beginning; for it is by their aid above all that we can imbibe the sound learning of the ancients, which is our chief aim and goal.

'In the name of good learning I entreat you with all instance not to abandon your plan of establishing the study of Greek in a secure home in Oxford. And as I cannot come to you, nor can your young men get leave to visit me, the only thing is for you to master the language for yourself. If you take my advice, you will go on with it at once and lose no opportunity that presents itself. You will not find it difficult, since you have already made a beginning, which is half the battle; and the rest you will soon master, for there is no better way of learning than to have to teach. But however difficult it might be, you cannot hesitate. It has long been your wish to become learned, and without Greek no one can hope for such a style; and the true learning that you seek is acknowledged by all to be enshrined in the wisdom of the Greeks. Your toil will become light and amusing, and your progress sure, if only you will read a little Lucian every day. Nor must your age deter you; remembering Marcus Cato, who began Greek when he was an old man, or that Euridice of Illyria, who, as Plutarch tells us, commenced scholar when her children had grown up. I copy out her epigram for you to read.

'Your state as priest forbids you to enjoy the happiness of having children of your own. In their place you may adopt the bright young intellects to whom you will be teaching Greek.

'To Master John Claymond, President of Magdalen College, Oxford.'

The dearth of trained men appears from a letter of Latimer who, when invited in 1517 to go and teach Fisher Greek at Rochester for a time, could only suggest that some one should be brought over from Italy for the purpose. The only Englishman of any attainment, who might have been secured for Fox and Wolsey, was Richard Croke, who had taught with success abroad, at Louvain and Cologne and Leipzig, 1515–17; but in 1518 he had been snapped up by his own University of Cambridge, for the lectureship in Greek, which Erasmus had once held. The same difficulty beset Francis' Collège de France, and indeed delayed its opening for some years; and as we shall see, the trilingual college at Louvain was for a long time no better off.

Another point of interest about the English foundations of this period is their attraction to foreigners. We are apt to think of travel as a speciality of the last three-quarters of a century, because of the facilities for speed offered to us in that period; and so I suppose it is, for the generality of mankind. But the student, British or foreign, like the man of commerce, has never been to hold or to bind. Ever since the Moorish schools in Spain, from the twelfth century onward, attracted students from all over Europe, there has been a continual flow and counterflow in all directions. The records of the different 'nations' at continental universities give abundant evidence of this; and it must be remembered that a great part of this student travelling was done on foot, for not many were rich enough to save shoe-leather by riding. As an example of the readiness with which men travelled, Ximenes invited scholars from Paris to attend the opening of Alcalá University, on the 18th of October 1508; and Charles Bouelles went down from Paris for the ceremony as we should go down for a ceremony at Leeds or Manchester. The journey from Paris to Alcalá must have occupied about a fortnight. Couriers could go from Vallodolid to Brussels or Antwerp in eleven days.

In the fifteenth century the Scotch thronged the University of Paris, and with their national passion for philosophy rose to the highest eminence in the schools. About 1500 More was almost the only English scholar of note who had not completed his studies abroad. The name of a student from a remote but unmistakable Oxfordshire village, Joannes de Duns Tew, appears in the matriculation register at Bologna. Leonard Cox of Reading became a schoolmaster in Hungary early in the sixteenth century. Wherever you turn, you may gather instances of Englishmen studying abroad. Examples of the contrary process are not equally abundant, as we had less to offer: Telamonius Limperger, a native of Mainz, who became later suffragan bishop of Basle, was sent by his order, the Augustinians, to study in London in 1477, but returned home because the climate was too bad, and went instead to Bologna. Cornelius Agrippa, on the contrary, came to London in 1510, not to study but on diplomatic business; and was delighted to find how much he could learn from Colet. The trilingual colleges of Cambridge and Oxford offered further attractions. Erasmus advised Reuchlin to send Melanchthon to work in Fisher's new foundation at St. John's. Two of Wolsey's early Readers were foreigners:

Vives the Spaniard whom we have mentioned, and Nicholas Kratzer of Munich, the mathematician and astronomer.

Another name that is not generally known in this connexion is Gentian Hervet of Orleans, afterwards of some prominence as a theologian at the Council of Trent. In a rare volume of *Orations* (presented by Bywater to the Bodleian) he mentions that at the age of nearly fourteen he came over with Lupset to England about 1519–20, and spent two years with him in Corpus —perhaps sharing his room and sleeping on the truckle-bed which was wheeled under the big bed by day, according to the arrangement prescribed by Fox in his Statutes for Fellow and scholar to share the same room. Hervet's connexion with England lasted long, for he left Oxford to become tutor to Reginald Pole, afterwards Cardinal, and was for nine years attached to the Pole family. A fruit of this long stay was that he became English enough to translate into our language a small treatise of Erasmus, *De immensa Dei misericordia*, twice printed in London about 1533.

The founder of the third trilingual college that we are to consider belonged to a Luxembourg family which had done well in Burgundian service. Jerome Busleiden was the third son, and of his elder brothers, Gilles held various important offices of finance under the government, and Francis became archbishop of Besançon. Jerome's tastes were for scholarship and a quiet life rather than administration, and instead of seeking a bishopric he collected several canonries, the archdeaconry of Cambray, the provostship of Aire, and finally the treasurership of St. Gudule's at Brussels in succession to his brother Francis, who had accompanied the Archduke Philip to Spain in 1501 and died the next year at

Toledo. The revenues of these posts enabled him to indulge his antiquarian instincts and pose as the patron of scholars: while their duties did not seriously interfere with his leisure. He built himself a fine house at Malines, which was the seat of one of his canonries; and among his pleasures were a rich library and a collection of coins. He evidently was a courtly person, of tact and with a good presence: for he was chosen to go on embassies of congratulation, first to Henry VIII and then to Francis I on their accessions—missions on which the first requisite was the power of being agreeable. He made friends with many scholars; Tunstall he had known when they were both studying in Italy, More visited him at Malines and wrote verses on his house and his coins, to Erasmus he was genuinely attached.

His literary output was small. A commendatory letter by him of empty compliment appeared in the first edition of More's *Utopia*; but otherwise practically nothing survives except a small collection of letters in manuscript, which unhappily are laboured and elegant rather than familiar, and as material for literary history are tantalizingly inexact, from a complete absence of dates.

After a good and useful life spent in this way he was chosen to accompany Charles to Spain in 1517, on the young prince's first visit after his grandfather Ferdinand's death. Spain had an ill fortune for the Burgundians and their followers. Besides the Archbishop of Besançon, the same visit had caused the death of the Archbishop of Cambray, who had barely strength to reach his home again before he succumbed; and a few years later the Archduke himself had died of a fever in Burgos. Jerome Busleiden's friends might well presage evil for him; and he had the foresight to make a detailed will, providing for the establishment of a trilingual college at the University of Brabant, Louvain. By a curious coincidence this will was signed on the 22nd of June 1517, only two days after Fox had given his Statutes at St. Cross for Corpus.

The first provision of interest in the will was as to the disposal of his body if he should die on the journey. If this event should occur before he reached the Pyrenees he wished to be brought back to Malines, where he had built himself a chapel in the cathedral; but if in Spain, he was to be laid with his brother Francis in the monastery of St. Bernard near Toledo. As it fell out, he almost reached the dividing line. On the 27th of August 1517 he died at Bordeaux; and the poor body was trundled back all across France before it found rest.

The bulk of his fortune he assigned to his College, which was to be of the following curious form. It was to consist of a President, who was also to be receptor or bursar, and manage the internal economy; three professors for the three languages, and eight (afterwards ten) students, who were to receive endowment. He wished this little community to be established *within* one of the existing colleges, either St. Donatian's or the College of Arras; but it is not surprising that so singular a proposal was promptly rejected by the authorities of each of the colleges concerned, and so after some hesitation the executors were obliged to give the new institution a separate home with buildings of its own.

The eight students, or scholars as we should call them, were allocated to districts with which Busleiden was connected just like the county system of scholarships and fellowships at Oxford and Cambridge. They were to give evidence of poverty before they could receive their stipends, twenty-five Rhenish florins a year each,

and they were to be over thirteen. They were to follow
the Arts course up to their M.A., until then only hearing
lectures from the Greek and Hebrew professors on Sun-
days and feast-days, the Latin Professor being generally
at their disposal for help with that tongue.

The three professors were to lecture publicly on Christian and moral authors, and were forbidden to take fees
from their audience, unless some distinguished ecclesiastic or nobleman should be there and wish for the sake
of his own credit to make a present to the lecturer—
such presents to be pooled and divided among the professors. The attendance of royalty at lectures was no
uncommon thing. When the Court was at Abingdon in
1518, Catherine of Aragon heard lectures in Oxford; and
Vives' lectures in Corpus a few years later are said to have
been attended by both King and Queen. Charles V sat
once upon the benches of Louvain: and so too in 1599
Albert and Isabella, the lady who has given her name to
the colour, to hear the erudition of Justus Lipsius. On
such occasions a royal present to the lecturer was no
doubt forthcoming. Busleiden's professors might also give
private tuition, and receive payment for it. The salaries
fixed for the three throw light on the position of the
market: and also indicate that Busleiden had ideas
about making a bargain. The Latin professor was to
receive besides his commons (*bursa* or *mensae portio*)
£6 Flemish a year; but the Greek and Hebrew were
each to have £12 a year, Busleiden judging—as was
the case—that it would be difficult to find qualified
professors, and thinking that high pay might tempt
them from other universities. After ten years, however,
their salary was to be reduced to £8: for by that time
it might be expected that there would be more trained
men available. The outgoing professors might be re-

tained at the lower pay, if they wished to stay on, provided it could be shown that they were still working hard. The money saved was to be used in founding two new scholarships.

As in Oxford, the first appointments were not men of distinction. Adrian Barlandus and Conrad Goclenius, the first Latinists, were respectable scholars: but at the dates of their appointment had produced very little. For the Greek chair there was great difficulty. At the request of the executors Erasmus wrote to John Lascaris, asking him to find a native Greek: but none was forthcoming and, in default of better, they had to appoint a young man named Rutger Rescius, from the neighbourhood of Liège. He held the chair for nearly thirty years, with sufficient distinction to be invited (without accepting) to transfer himself to the Collège de France at Paris in 1527. In Hebrew the executors had even less success. Their first choice was a converted Jew named Matthew Adrianus, who wrote dreadful Latin: but after a year an oration which he delivered, so roused the theologians that he found it wiser to retire to Wittenberg. Then followed two young Englishmen, Robert Wakefeld and Robert Shirwood, whose tenure of office was very brief; one for four months, the other for one. And it was not till Campensis, who held the chair from 1520 to 1531, that there was any fixity; and he was wishing to be gone within a few years of his appointment.

The first professors were appointed in 1518, and began lecturing in the hall of the Austin Friars at Louvain; and it was not before October 1520 that the college was established in buildings of its own—the idea of its being established within another college having proved impracticable.

For the actual working of the college the material

available is all too scanty. In 1521 a senior Fellow of St. John's at Cambridge, one Nicholas Darynton, went over to Louvain to study; though he gives plenty of information about his life there, he does not mention the trilingual college. But his letter is amusing and worth quoting.

'The theological exercises here give me very little entertainment. The lectures are slow, the disputations are slow, everything is very genteel—which I should approve of, if only it weren't so dull and such solemn trifling. Very different from Paris, where the Sorbonnists shout at one another, foaming at the mouth and gnashing their teeth.'

He found the food disagreeable, fat and soaked in butter —probably the kind of stuff that exhales from fried fish shops in this country, or what in India is known as *ghi*.

'My studies', he continues, 'are carried on alone; except that I go to hear a Spaniard named Vives lecturing on Mela; and he has also expounded to us Suetonius' life of Julius Caesar. But in one way it is much easier to study here than in Cambridge; for there are none of those tiresome visits of formality, none of the backbiting and discussion of others, the canvassing for offices and pursuit of votes by all means fair or foul, while the conduct of the University is neglected.'

Another letter which refers to Busleiden's College is from Ascham to Edward Raven, written at Augsburg, 20 January 1551.

At Louvain, 11 a.m. to 2 p.m., 6th October 1550.

'I went to P. Nannius' chamber, to have talked with him; but he was either drunken at home or drinking abroad: for he was making merry and would not be seen, as an English boy, his pupil, told me. He reads Tully's Orations at nine of the clock.

'At one of the clock Theodoricus Laudius read (whom I heard) Oed. Tyr. Sophocl. graece. He read that chiding place betwixt

Oedipus and Creon, beginning at οὐκ οἶδ᾽· ἐφ᾽ οἷς γὰρ μὴ φρονῶ σιγᾶν φιλῶ, ⟨569⟩ reading twenty-one verses. His hearers, being about eighty, did knock him out with such an noise as I have not heard.

'This college is called Trilingue et Buslidianum, where he read. If Louvain, as far as I could mark, were compared with Cambridge, Trilingue with St. John's or Trinity College, Theod. Laudius with Mr. Car, ours do far excel.

'The reader in οι followed our pronounciation. I tarried so long at his lecture that my lord ⟨the ambassador⟩ was ridden out of the town.'

The path of the college in its early days was not smooth. The professors began by annoying the Arts Faculty, by claiming injudiciously the right to teach without receiving authorization from the University: a claim they were quite unable to maintain. At the same time the theologians attacked their whole position, contending that the laborious acquisition of Hebrew and Greek was unnecessary for any of the studies of the University. The most brilliant of them, Latomus, whom Luther regarded as the most dangerous of all his opponents, produced a dialogue on the subject: to which Erasmus had no difficulty in making an adequate reply. On the general question Erasmus was prepared to concede that Greek should not be required of every theologian; but he insisted that those who chose thus to remain in ignorance of the original of the New Testament must know their place.

One of Latomus' arguments is interesting, as showing the standard that the education of the day set before itself. 'How impossible', he says, 'that people should spend their time on Greek. It takes a man seven years to learn to speak tolerable Latin. Are they to give another seven years to Greek?' Clearly therefore a complete command of these dead languages, to speak as well as to write, was of the highest importance to them. Though translation into the vernaculars was beginning, a remark of Erasmus in controverting Latomus' view, shows how little use was made of them in the writings of the learned: 'It would be generally admitted', he says, 'that a man might be able to write with some correctness about divinity, even if he knew no language but English'. But in fact at the beginning of the sixteenth century, such audacity had scarcely begun. It was not till the Reformers began to appeal to a wider circle than the learned, and to find allies in the people against conservatism entrenched in Church and State, that there arose the use of the vernacular for serious writing, in which the learned might be interested.

A consideration which presents itself is this. How far did the patrons of this movement expect to make education trilingual? Busleiden's provision that his scholars should first go through the M.A. course seems to imply that he at least had no such expectation: though he contemplated such an extension of Hebraists and Grecists as would enable his chairs to be filled at a lower cost. Fox, as we saw, provided for Divinity rather than Hebrew. Yet, as the researches of Professor Watson show, the great schoolmasters of a century later in this country, Brinsley and Hoole, regarded Hebrew as a school subject. In the remote village of Martock in Somerset you may see the remains of a trilingual school founded in 1661, with an inscription over the door in Hebrew and Greek and Latin.

CHRISTOPHER PLANTIN
AND HIS CIRCLE

A MASTER printer is apt to become a Maecenas if he have a taste that way. For himself what is needed is the technical knowledge of his art and the princely habit, in happy combination with the capacity for doing good business. To foster art and learning may be easy and congenial for a great patron with the wealth of Church or State behind him: less easy when the fosterer must coax from the purse of the book-buying public the lucre by which men of art and learning may live. Thus the two roles, of patron and printer, were often separate. The famous Cardinal of Spain, Ximenes, endowing his young University of Alcalá with the printer Brocario; Giberti at Verona, with the presses of the Sabii established in his episcopal palace; Sir Henry Savile bringing the London printer Norton to work under his hand at Eton—these are examples of what wealth and munificence can achieve. To combine the two parts is more difficult; and of those who succeed, history is not forgetful. Gutenberg at Mainz and Fust with his disciples who were soon, under the cruel blows of war, to carry the new art into all lands; Asulanus and Aldus at Venice, filling their big house with scholars and founding a New Academy; Amorbach and Froben at Basle with their high ambitions of patristic learning, and the presses toiling to keep up with Erasmus' pen; the Kobergers at Nuremberg; Jodocus Badius in Paris—such great names as these must have been often in Plantin's mind; though, for all his adventurous spirit, he can hardly have hoped ever to emulate them.

The citizen whom Antwerp delights to honour, the

famous printer—who may almost be described as only a printer by accident—was a Frenchman, born in the village of St. Avertin, near Tours. His mother dying early, he was carried away to Lyons by his father, who had obtained service there with the canon in charge of the Church of St. Just. After some years his father took him to Paris to complete his education, and then went off himself to Toulouse, leaving the boy a small sum of money and promising to send for him soon. Nothing more was heard of him, and the young Christopher was thrown on his own resources. His enterprising temperament at once rose to the emergency. Making his way to Caen, he apprenticed himself to a printer, Robert Macé; and having learnt the arts which go to the making of a book, in 1545–6 he married Jeanne Rivière, a portionless girl who was serving in his master's household, and went off with her to seek their fortunes in Paris.

In 1549 they moved to Antwerp, and Plantin began to practise the art he had chosen for his livelihood, that of bookbinding and other leather work. He prospered quickly, and the world went well. Then one evening, as he was carrying home a finished box to a Spanish secretary of Philip II, a wound, from a blow aimed at another, maimed one of his hands for ever and turned him back— a middle-aged man with a nursery of young children—to the printer's art he had deliberately forsaken. In 1555 his books began to appear—thin octavos at first, many of them pirated as the custom of the age allowed; and he was embarked upon the bold career which was to lead him to fame. Books of travel appear to have had special attraction for him. Leo Africanus, pirated, was one of his earliest selections; then Alvarez' *Ethiopia* and Olaus Magnus on the *Nations of the North*.

It was no light venture. He had been attracted to

Antwerp by the number of its printers, long-established firms whose abundant output offered opportunities to the binder. With these he had now to compete, and every available member of his family was pressed into the service. 'It has pleased God', he wrote in 1570, 'to leave me no son living in this world.' But his four eldest daughters, born between 1547 and 1557, 'from the age of four or five until they were twelve, each one of them, according to her years and standing, helped me to read the proofs sent from the press, in whatever handwriting and in any tongue.' Fit helpmates thus they became—since their good French mother had taught them the use of the needle and all the resources of the housewife's craft— for the young men who, coming to write their father's Latin letters and serve him at the correctors' table, stayed to be his sons-in-law. For a time the firm made good progress, and settled into more ample quarters, at the Golden Compass in the Kammerstraet, whose emblem appears on so many of his title-pages. Then in 1561 came a new blow, this time directed at himself. He was suspected of leanings towards heresy; and for nearly two years he was a fugitive in Paris, leaving wife and children to the care of friends. The grounds for the charge seem to have been his connexion with the Family of Charity, one of those associations which are ever being formed anew, in all ages and in all lands, by men who seek to lead a godly, righteous, and sober life, and which are independent of established religion. This mystic Family, the creation of Henry Niclaes, a Westphalian now wandering through the Netherlands, was based upon the love of man in obedience to the will of God. As this prime duty was common to all men of goodwill, Niclaes taught that to be his disciple none should leave the religion in which he had been brought up, and that the Family should permeate, not supplant. No dreadful doctrine this; but in those dark days of anxiety the orthodox quaked at any shadow of turning; and Plantin found safety in flight.

Returning in 1563 he bought back such of his confiscated property as friends had been able to secure for him by purchase in their own names. With his habitual courage he launched out into new schemes. The Catholic King, to buttress up the faith, wished for a new edition of the Bible which should be an improvement on the earlier Polyglott of which Spain was proud, the Complutensian, produced for Cardinal Ximenes in his young university at Alcalá. After some negotiations Plantin secured the contract. Philip sent over one of his chaplains to serve as editor. New type was cast, the finest paper was ordered from Auvergne, and for six special copies vellum at 100 florins the set.

Simultaneously with this great achievement, Plantin made another venture, which was to prove the foundation of his own wealth and that of his children's children. In 1568 he bought the Netherlands rights for the new Breviary which Pius V had had prepared in accordance with the decisions of the Council of Trent; and in 1570 he acquired the rights for the new Missal also, not only in the Netherlands but in Hungary and parts of Germany. The demand for these and for other books of devotion was, of course, enormous; and from the profits thus made he was able to finance some of the costly works of learning which could not pay their own way.

Plantin's helpers were many, foremost among them two of his sons-in-law. First Francis Raphelengien, born near Lille in 1539. His studies had received their foundation in Ghent, till at his father's death he was sent to earn his living on an office-stool in Nuremberg. From

such distasteful tasks he begged release, and was allowed
to go and learn Hebrew and Greek in Paris. For a while
he was in Cambridge, teaching Greek. Then in March
1564 he contracted to serve Plantin for two years, and
by Midsummer 1565 had welded himself to the family
for ever through taking Marguerite, the eldest daughter,
to wife. He remained at Plantin's right hand, working
upon one book after another, though his name appears
upon few title-pages. His great interest was for Oriental
languages. In the Polyglott he supervised the printing
of the Hebrew and the Syriac, and revised Paganinus'
Hebrew dictionary for inclusion in it. When he moved
with Plantin to Leyden, the University hastened to
make him its Professor of Hebrew, 1586–7; and at his
death in 1597 he was still compiling an Arabic lexicon,
which his sons and Marguerite's published in 1613.

Next to him came Jean Moretus, born at Antwerp in
1543. He entered Plantin's service in the early days, at
the age of fourteen, obviously in some humble capacity.
When Plantin had to fly to Paris in 1561, Moretus went
off to Venice in quest of experience. Returning in 1565
he became increasingly useful in the counting-house, and
in 1570 was rewarded with the hand of Plantin's second
daughter, Martine. Plantin describes him then as knowing Greek and Latin as well as Spanish, Italian, French,
German, and Flemish—the modern languages acquired
of course for business purposes. It was on this side that
he was strong; it was not his to see what a great press
can do for learning. When at Plantin's death he took over
the management of it, a change comes over its output.
Scientific works, especially those of any size, grow fewer;
and the strength of the house goes into those safe undertakings, books of liturgy and devotion, for which there
is a constant sale and a sure return into the firm's money-

bags, maintenance for wife and children and all the many dependents of a great establishment. Yet there was one exception, one friend for whom he would venture anything, many of whose works he published, the famous scholar Justus Lipsius. This side of his character appears in the one piece of literary work that he did himself, a translation into Flemish (1584) of Lipsius' *De Constantia*. Others who worked in Plantin's house were the brothers Guy and Nicholas le Fèvre de la Boderie; John Isaac, a Jew of Cologne; Andrew Madoets, charged with the care of a new edition of Froissart, never completed; Gilles Beys, who in 1571 married Magdelaine, Plantin's fourth daughter, and became head of a branch in Paris.

Besides these, scholars came from afar; and beyond was the extended company of those who brought their books for him to publish. Of the first, the best known is Benedict Arias Montanus (1527–98): his surname derived from the mountains among which he was born, Fregenal de la Sierra in Estremadura. A student at Seville and Alcalá, the home of Ximenes' Polyglott, he retired at the age of twenty-five into his native mountains of Aracena, to devote himself as a recluse to the monumental accumulation of learning. From this he was drawn forth by zeal for the faith. In 1560 he joined the Order of Santiago, one of those great military fraternities through which Spain had warded off and at length repelled the infidel; and in 1562 he suffered himself to be carried off by the Bishop of Segovia, interested like himself in Hebrew studies, to assist at the last deliberations of the Council of Trent. Contact with the world opened to him new opportunities. A friend from Venice showed him a manuscript which had come over from Constantinople, that home where the Jews had found shelter under the Turk and were printing their books, safe from Christian persecution. The manuscript was the Itinerary of the twelfth-century Jew, Benjamin of Tudela in Navarre. Arias showed it to his Bishop, and was encouraged to make a Latin translation; of which Plantin afterwards published (1575) the first edition. From this time onwards Arias' ears were open to any news of manuscripts from afar—fit preparation for one who was later to lay the foundations of his master's library at the Escurial. He might retire to Aracena again, but there was no more seclusion for him. In 1568 Philip, who had recently appointed him his chaplain, sent him a mandate, bidding him emerge to work with Plantin upon the new Polyglott that was to be a still richer armoury for defenders of the Faith. To such a call Arias could not be deaf. Those bright little Spanish eyes show no trace of hesitation or fear, though he was to pass through perils by sea. His ship was cast away on the west coast of Ireland, and he had to cross the water twice again before arriving at Antwerp in May. The lines of the great undertaking were soon drawn, he was established in his own house, and Magdelaine Plantin, aged twelve, ran to and fro, carrying him the proofs. When the eight folio volumes were at length complete in 1572, with richly engraved title-pages and duly fortified with privileges, Arias crowned his labours with a mighty preface, in which he reveals what manner of man he was. After discussing mankind's place among the animals, his opportunities and his proneness to evil, he deplores the sad tares of error and schism which that ancient adversary, the Devil, has sown in the fair fields of truth and wisdom; the wickedness of modern translators, who have presumed to reject the Vulgate; and the woeful horrors of those turbulent days—a note which is repeated over and over again in the prefaces of Plantin's books. The seven years that he dwelt at Antwerp forged close ties between him and the printer; and the letters which they exchanged after he had returned to Spain are very human documents. It would be interesting to know whether Arias had any inkling of his friend's connexion with the Family of Charity.

The books which Plantin printed represent not merely the learning therein contained, but all the wide and varied experience of their authors. In producing their writings to the world, he at the same time drew into his city the sum of the knowledge they had collected and the new ideas that arose out of it. Amid the busy hum of commerce, ever opening up new worlds, new realms of thought also were being illumined; and from their welling sources Plantin gave to his contemporaries drink as out of the river. Yet one wonders how much heed was paid in that busy city by the merchants in their offices or the shipmen on the wharves, to the shy and quiet scholars making their way into Plantin's presence and asking acceptance of the fruits of their labours. He himself, in spite of temporary reverses, was on the whole a rich man, furnished with ability, such as the world can understand; but of what went on within his walls, of all those active brains and hands that he employed, the men of Antwerp very likely recked little and spoke less, just as to-day men are commonly too occupied to bestow a thought upon what is not obvious before their eyes.

The infinite variety which lies behind the plainest human life is often much enhanced for those who give their years to study, seeking not for themselves, things new and old, at any cost of danger and adventure. To take an example—a single life considered in detail may be more suggestive than a briefer treatment of many— the celebrated botanist Clusius, one of Plantin's band, born at Arras as Jules Charles de l'Escluse (1526–1609). Much had he seen and known before he offered his first book to the new printing-house at Antwerp. He had learnt his classics at Ghent, and in Busleiden's College at Louvain. He had studied law at Marburg; and at Wittenberg, sitting at Melanchthon's feet he had become a firm Protestant. Then to Montpellier, where he was attracted into the study of nature, and made his first essay into it by translating into Latin the treatise of his adored teacher Rondelet, on the Fishes of the Sea. Taking pupils to maintain himself, he was for a year or two at Paris and Louvain with two young Redigers from Breslau, afterwards to become famous as antiquaries, under his inspiration, and endow their native town. Then to Spain with some young Fuggers, 'only, for eight months' he says apologetically, when announcing his discoveries. Two hundred species of flowers he found, including choice narcissus from the plains of Toledo and the hill-sides near Cadiz: not without bruises and broken bones, as he fell from rocky ledges, or when his horse stumbled on the stony ways. Besides his flowers he brought other treasures, copies of the Roman inscriptions in which Spain is rich; the manuscripts from which Plantin printed that second fascinating volume of the letters of Clenardus—a man of whom Clusius always writes with profound veneration—the bold scholar of Diest, who twenty-five years before had penetrated into Morocco and as far as Fez, in pursuit of the language and learning of the Arabs. Other sides of Clusius' interests appear in his translations: an account of the spices of the East Indies, from the Portuguese; two of Plutarch's Lives, out of the Latin, which he contributed to the great French Plutarch of Amyot, bishop of Auxerre.

Clusius could not rest long at home, even with Plan-

tin's press at hand, and with his friend Dodonaeus at
Malines. In 1571–2 he was in England, talking to our
botanists Penny and Lyte; ten years later he was there
again, interviewing Drake. In 1573 the Emperor invited
him to Vienna, where for some years he enjoyed the
company of Dodonaeus—also an Imperial protégé, and
of Ogier de Busbecq, Imperial librarian, who as Ambassador to the Terrible Turk had read the monument of
Ancyra and had brought back to Europe the lilac and
the tulip. During his first years Clusius sent back to
Plantin an account of the simples which grow in the
West Indies, and the record of the flowers he had seen
in Spain. Then when a new Emperor made life hard for
Protestants he wandered off into Hungary and found
shelter in the castle of a count, while he gathered
material for a new Plantin volume on the flora of that
side of Europe. Returning at length to the north, he
too like Raphelengien ended his life holding a chair—of
course of Botany—at Leyden.

This is but one example of the rich and varied lives
of the men who found their centre in Plantin, while his
ability enabled them to lay their riches at the service
of their own day and of posterity. There were many
others, no less interesting than Clusius. Such were Arias'
staff for the Polyglott; Lindanus, bishop of Roermond,
and the Louvain theologians; Pamelius and all those
learned doctors who brought out the Augustine, and
the Jerome; Antonio of Siena, a Portuguese Dominican,
eager to edit Thomas Aquinas; John Goropius Becanus,
who had accompanied the two Queens as physician when
they followed Charles V into his retirement in Spain,
author of that surprising book the *Origines Antwerpianae*; Hadrian Junius, physician to our Duke of Norfolk
and later to the King of Denmark, the first to put

forward in his *Batauia* the claim of Haarlem to be the home
of printing; the botanists, Dodonaeus of Malines who
was physician to the Emperor at Vienna, and Lobel of
Lille, eponymous 'inventor' of that little blue flower,
which to some gardening minds is as inseparably connected with red geraniums as Jenny Wren of the poets
is with Robin Redbreast, Ortelius, the geographer;
Turnebus and Justus Lipsius, Pulmannus and William
Canter, classical scholars; Stephen Pighius and Gerard
Falkenburg, antiquarians and students of inscriptions;
Peter Bizarius, historian of Persia; Duarenus and
Raeuardus, lawyers; Alan Cope and Nicholas Harps-
field from England; George Buchanan from Scotland;
Richard Stanyhurst, refugee from Ireland; Fulvio Orsini
from Rome; Hosius and Duditius from Cracow; Sanctius
Brocensis from Salamanca. All their light and learning
was brought together by Plantin's genius as to a focus,
to be increased and multiplied and diffused again where-
ever men could read.

Plantin's character must be read in his letters, of which
there are seven delightful volumes. He appears as a keen
man of business, cautious with all his boldness, and not
to be imposed upon in matters of trade. Most attractive
is he when he writes of his family or to them. The memo-
randum of 1570 for Philip's secretary gives an intimate
picture of them all, mother and daughters and the grand-
children whose voices were already heard in the great
house. Another letter, addressed to his third daughter,
Catherine, just gone as a bride of eighteen to dwell in
her father-in-law's house in Paris, shows him as a plain,
God-fearing man, with no illusions about the success
which he had won *labore et constantia*.

'Consider', he writes, 'that neither you nor I nor your husband
are of any different flesh from the least people that dwell upon

this earth. If God has given us quicker wits or better judgment than some others, He has not done it for love of us, nor for our beaux yeux as the saying goes. It is not a thing to be proud of as if it were our own, but it is for the glory of God and that we may be able to aid and support the ignorant folk prudently with all our power.'

It is well to recall the conditions under which Plantin's work was done, the 'turbulent times' which the prefaces in his books continually deplore. The political hostility of the Netherlands towards Philip was aggravated by the growth of religious dissension. Luther and Calvin had found many disciples there, and these looked for their leader to the Prince of Orange instead of to the Catholic King. In 1566, just when Plantin, returned from Paris, was beginning to feel firm again upon his feet, a Protestant rising swept over the country, violating churches and slaying monks before their altars. Philip replied by sending Alva; and the Council of Blood pro-ceeded, like Saul, to slay its thousands. Persecution only embittered the opposition, and the whole country seethed with public anarchy and private feuds. On 4 November 1576 Antwerp was ravaged by the 'Spanish Fury', an outbreak of soldiers clamouring for their pay. Nine times during that night Plantin was held to ransom in his own house, and nine times appeased his captors with gold— more fortunate than the 7,000 victims who had nothing to offer in exchange for their lives. No wonder that he bethought him of the invitations he kept receiving from his master Philip, from the King of France, and from the Duke of Savoy. In 1583, leaving his new house on the Marché du Vendredi and accompanied by Francis Raphelengien, he moved his press to Leyden, already standing out as the home of freedom of thought; only to return in 1585 to spend his last days in the

Antwerp which he had chosen for his home forty years before.

At his death in 1589 the business was divided in the main between Raphelengien, still printing at Leyden, and John Moretus. But change came rapidly on. Raphelengien was a scholar, absorbed in Arabic studies; Moretus was primarily a man of business. The only one of Plantin's successors to be like him was his grandson Balthasar Moretus (1574–1641), son of John and Martine, the schoolfellow of Rubens and the pupil of Justus Lipsius. Paralysed on one side from his birth, through his mother's fright 'at the time of the first troubles', he was marked out for the scholar's sedentary life. Entering the house in 1598 as writer of its Latin letters, he brought to it later, when at its head, the spirit of his grandfather for splendid undertakings without counting too narrowly the cost. Works of learning again predominate. Inspired by his schoolfellow, he completed the beautiful quadrangle which all good printers go to visit on the Marché du Vendredi, and by his will secured it as an indivisible property.

In the hands of the next generations the Officina Plantiniana leaned more and more on the service books. Through later centuries these were its staple production, till at last they alone kept it alive, to pass in 1876 into the possession of the City of Antwerp as the Musée Plantin-Moretus.

In conclusion, two extracts about the great city and province in which Plantin worked may be quoted from books which he published. Contemporary description, written by men who were just as modern in their own judgement as we seem to ourselves to be to-day, has always a vivid power of illumination. The first is from Goropius' *Origines Antwerpianae*, 1569.

'The citizens of Antwerp are of a pleasing simplicity and lightness of heart, which lasts with them to the extreme of old age;
indeed the Brabançon gaiety has become a proverb. In consequence no city shows greater hospitality to foreigners, and to
none do they more freely resort. Among themselves, life is
bright and happy, with ready wit, pleasant stories, music and
song and dance. It is a handsome city with splendid streets, fine
and comfortable houses, elegant furniture. Round it are agreeable suburbs, with magnificent mansions fit for kings, standing
in gardens rich with every kind of shrub and flower. In search
of sound learning the inhabitants wander far and wide. Every
educated man among them has at his command three, four and
five languages, and some have even more; and these they speak
with the utmost skill, making mistake neither in word nor in
pronunciation.'

The second passage comes from Lobel's preface to his
Plantarum Historia, printed by Plantin in 1576:

'This fair Gallo-Belgic Province, known to the ancients as
Flanders or Lower Germany, is now the busy mart of all Europe,
whither are brought in abundance the rarities of all the world,
the wealth of Europe, Asia and Africa. Its northern climate,
with long winters and bitter frosts, with fierce gales and in-
clement weather, is ill-suited for the rearing of plants. But the
industry of the inhabitants and the pains they take to shelter the
young growth, have overcome these obstacles, and Belgian
gardeners are in my opinion to be esteemed above all others.
Here are to be found more variety of plants and trees than in
ancient Greece, broad Spain, Germany, England, France and
even highly cultivated Italy.'

Among renowned owners of gardens at that time he
names Charles de Croy, prince of Chimay; Pierre de
Bossu, lord of Jeumont; Charles de Bossu, viscount
of Brussels; Gilbert d'Oignies, bishop of Tournai; Jean
de Branchion; Charles de Houchin, lord of Longastre;
Jean Boisot; Jacques Utenhove; Philippe Deurnagle,
lord of Vroyland; Jean de Limoges; and he extols also

Clusius and the royal professors at Louvain, Pierre de Breughel, Cornelius Gemma, and Jean Viringus.

'These last', he goes on, 'have helped me very much in my work, and have shown me many rare plants which they have had brought for their gardens from Constantinople, Greece, Spain, Italy, Asia, Africa and the New Found World. Also they have provided me with many herbs, which I had sent them before, from Italy, Provence and Languedoc; the seeds of which I had lost in the disturbances at Lyons. The present book is published as a record of what remain to me, lest they too should perish in these deplorable times.'

ERASMIAN WAYFARINGS

ALCALÁ

A SPANISH COLLEGIUM TRILINGUE

TWENTY miles to the east of Madrid lies the Roman city of Complutum, which is now known by its Moorish name, Al-Calá, the castle. At the turn of the fifteenth century it still had some importance. Catherine of Aragon was born there in 1485, Ferdinand the Emperor in 1503, Cervantes in 1547; and at its school was educated Jimenez de Cisneros, or Ximenes, the famous Cardinal Archbishop of Toledo. The town is pleasantly situated. To the south runs the Henares, at the foot of a low range of hills, whose steep soft cliffs and flat grass-capped tops form an unusual and striking effect. The plain rises slowly to the north, bright with green cornfields intersected by avenues of poplars and elms, and here and there a dark clump of cypresses, or the gay colour of the Judas tree, beside a house gleaming white in the sunshine. The view is wide, and in the distance, where the plain rises to a ridge, the long rampart of the Guadarrama mountains shines beyond, with top after top showing up along the northern horizon, thickly snow-covered even in May. And above all the blue of the southern sky.

In 1500 Ximenes was at the height of his power. His had been an eventful life. Six of his best years, thirty-seven to forty-three, had been spent in prison, as a result of a dispute with a superior over a benefice to which the Pope had presented him. After long austerities as an Observant, the strictest sect of the Franciscans, he had returned to the world, master of himself and fitted to become a master of others. He had attracted the notice of the Grand Cardinal Mendoza, Archbishop of Toledo, who in 1492 moved Isabella to choose him as her confessor, and on his death-bed urged the Queen to nominate him as his successor in the see of Toledo. Isabella assented, and thus in 1495 Ximenes reluctantly found himself, when within a year of sixty, Primate of Spain and master of enormous revenues.

One of his projects for the advancement of his country was to found a university, where the studies of the Renaissance should receive due consideration. The Spanish College founded at Bologna by Albornoz in 1364 had supplied a channel by which the new interests and ideas flowed into Spain; and there were now many scholars there of the first rank. The old universities, Salamanca and Palencia (merged with Salamanca in xiii^c), were not progressive; and Ximenes judged that royal Valladolid with the busy life of a Court was no place for a university, although two splendid colleges had only recently been built there—San Gregorio in 1488, and Santa Cruz in 1492. So for the site of his new institution his choice fell on the city he had known from his boyhood. In 1500 the building began, and in 1508 the University of Alcalá was ready to receive its first pupils. Its equipment was magnificent. Ten colleges had sprung up, and forty-two professors had been appointed to the various studies, old and new alike. One of the colleges was founded by the Archbishop of Santiago; but most were the creation of Ximenes, who, whenever he could escape from state business, rejoiced to visit and superintend the building. There was a printing press, in which Arnold of Brocario, transplanted from Pamplona, produced the great *Complutensian Polyglott*— the Bible in Hebrew, Greek, Latin, and Aramaic, six folio volumes. Ximenes had promoted the work; Leo X lent manuscripts from the Vatican; and the ablest scholars in Spain, Antonius Nebrissensis, John Vergara, Pincianus, Demetrios Doukas, and others, carried it out. The New Testament—printed for the first time in Greek—was completed in 1514, and the last sheets of the whole work were carried to Ximenes shortly before his death in 1517.

Since the University was transferred in 1836 from its peaceful seat to a dreary building in a noisy quarter of Madrid, Alcalá has declined. The colleges are put to other uses. One is a barrack, another an asylum, another a hospital. Only San Ildefonso, Ximenes' greatest creation, still serves some educational purposes. It stands on a small square, its imposing façade gleaming in the afternoon sun, whilst bugles sound and dismounted cavalry-men pass to and fro in their blue uniforms. The stone is pink or golden—it is hard to tell which hue prevails—and the broad front gives a sense of ample welcome and simplicity, avoiding alike the fantastic designs of San Gregorio at Valladolid and the richness of San Marcos at Leon. On knocking one is admitted by the guardian-porter to a quadrangle of grey granite, three-storied and at the top a balustrade, round which runs an inscription —confusing to read, because it is carved, a letter at a time, on the larger uprights—to say that this court which was once *lutea* was made *marmorea* in 1562. The date is scarcely needed, for the broad columns and heavy ornament show that in the day of its building the fine work of the Renaissance was giving place to the fullness of baroque. But the transformers were pious; and along the walls and cornices, on the fountain too in the centre, appear the arms and the swans of Cisneros, as the guardian invariably called him. One wing is given up to a primary school, and another is occupied by the 'Padres Esculapios', an order of medical clergy, who take good care of the home entrusted to them.

But the guardian leads on, into another court, spacious and open, as the buildings on three sides are low—seemingly all that remains of the original work, which, doubtless, was *luteum* as in the first court. An avenue of white acacias, smelling as sweet as oranges, leads across to another door; and, as we pass through, San Ildefonso stands revealed, a *Collegium trilingue*, with a quadrangle for each of the three languages.

Such was the desire of the age, to turn the studies of the universities back from the mazes of philosophy to the niceties of language and literature; and pious founders chose first the languages of the Bible, Hebrew and Greek and Latin. Ximenes' conception rapidly found imitators. To Cambridge the Lady Margaret, advised by Fisher, gave Christ's and St. John's. Rome itself had its College of Greek, founded by Leo X and guided by John Lascaris and Musurus. In Oxford Fox and Wolsey united in a scheme, one creating Corpus, the other bringing lecturers from across the sea, until his own Cardinal College was complete. For Paris Francis I projected the Collège de France; at Louvain, second only to Paris for its orthodoxy, the executors of Jerome Busleiden brought to birth a college which should perpetuate his name. Fonseca gave colleges to Santiago and Salamanca; and at Vienna Faber created the College of St. Nicholas. Many of these were definitely trilingual, Corpus perhaps among the number, if the study of Hebrew be regarded as implicit in Sacred Divinity, with which Fox's third 'gardener' was to nourish his 'bees': but all were deeply imbued with the spirit of the Renaissance.

San Ildefonso's third quadrangle greeted us with the scent of stocks that comes to meet those who on summer eves pass towards the Fellows' garden at Corpus. The buildings were low, but pure Renaissance work; a gal-

lery running round all four sides, supported by slender
columns with elegant medallions in the spandrils of the
arches, and forming a covered walk. Flowers filled the
whole court—roses and periwinkles, snapdragon and
peonies, and above all great bushes of the stocks. 'Good
for the bees,' said the guardian, to our astonishment: it
seemed almost as though he must have understood our
instant comparison with Corpus, the *Collegium apum*.
Out of this court opened the *Paraninfo*, a hall for lectures
and disputations—there was no sign of its ever having
been used for dining—with three raised seats for presid-
ing doctors, and two surrounding galleries, one a few feet
above the floor, the other at the top, outside the room
but giving sight of the hall, through richly ornate arches.
By dark dusty stairways we climbed to the higher gallery:
on the outer side its arches looked over a yard where the
Guardia Civil—that fine body of men that have rid Spain
of brigandage—were playing at ball against the wall of
Ximenes' College. But their full powers have bred awe
in quiet spirits—a light price to pay for peace—the
guardian begged us not to be seen looking at them in
their ease.

At one corner of the gallery we pushed a door open,
and there indeed were the bees. San Ildefonso, too, was
a *Collegium apum*! Their hives were full, and many of
the honey-laden workers were crawling over the floor.
'Their majesties will be pleased not to walk upon them,'
said the guardian; and his words carried us once more
back to Corpus, to think of the late President walking in
his garden—almost his last walk—and saying, 'There's
one of those dear bees; don't kill it.'

Ximenes' chapel is still used by the primary school,
and beds of flowers surround the approach to it; but
when the guardian led us back to the college gate, to

direct us to Ximenes' tomb in the *Yglesia magistral*, we
were almost surprised to find ourselves still in Spain.

A CASTLE IN SPAIN

As the *rapido* drew out, the people in the corridors of
the last carriages seemed surprised at the sight of two
obvious foreigners left standing at such a wayside station.
Our first care was to register the luggage on by the afternoon train to Valladolid: for in Spain it may not travel
without you, however soon you are to follow. By the
time the obliging station-master had achieved our desire
—'Balyadolee' he seemed to pronounce the destination
—the stir caused by the passage of the *rapido* had settled
down again. The noonday sun shone out of a clear blue
on the fireman of a goods train who was returning from
replenishing his bottle at the wine-shop outside the
station-yard—the only house to be seen in any direction.
But for the black figure stepping across the lines and the
impatient hissing of his engine, southward bound to
Madrid but held up interminably in a siding, the world
might have been asleep.

After a visit to the wine-shop, which for 2½*d.* flowed
with streams of thin red wine, we sallied forth for the
walk of two miles to Coca. The object of our quest was
uncertain. In describing the route on from Segovia,
Baedeker halts to mention the castle of Coca, and his
guiding star indicates 'Tombs of the Fonsecas'. We had
been reading in Madrid the autograph letters of Alonso
de Fonseca, archbishop of Toledo and Primate of Spain,
who continued at Alcalá the liberal patronage of its
founder, his sometime predecessor, Ximenes. Fonseca
tombs and a Fonseca castle might yield something; at
any rate it seemed worth while to miss a train or two
and go to see.

The heat was dry and hard: just pleasant to sit still in, almost—but not quite—uncomfortable when one began to move. The road disappeared into a sparse forest of stone-pines; short trees cut into trim shapes and casting pools of thin shade, and each with its pot into which resin was draining. From pool to pool we wound our way over the sunburnt grass, the strewn pine-needles making our footsteps noiseless. Now and then flashed past a butterfly, whose blues and browns seemed almost a conscious imitation of the landscape; or a hoopoe alighted with a whirring wave of its crest. At a bend came into view the only party that was to share the road with us—His Majesty's mails. It was a small company: a donkey with a slip of a boy riding on its quarters, and across its saddle a thin sack striped with the crimson and gold of Spain, and scarcely a peseta's worth of letters in it, even at $1\frac{1}{2}d.$ each. Beside them marched a girl of a year or two older, holding an umbrella to protect her bare head. It appeared afterwards that she belonged to the wine shop: so that the majesty of Castile and Leon and Aragon was represented by the animal and its rider alone. Hence perhaps the want of chivalry.

The road descended a steep sandy bank to a river; then across an unshaded bridge and up a burning gully. At the top a little breeze allured us to sit in such shade as could be found and survey Coca. In front stood the castle rising into tower and walls of rose-pink brick: away to one side stretched part of the town wall, still showing the arch of a gate, beside which at an unpromising *posada* a muleteer was loading his packs: further off lay a line of modern workshops, a centre of some activity, which had perhaps given its slender substance to the mail-sack. Near at hand a sturdy sun-dried fellow was burning bricks in a kiln, regardless of heat and the temptation to siesta.

The structure of the castle was simple—a central tower standing in a court and protected by strong walls. But its feature was the *cubos*, small brick bastions creeping down the corners of the walls and tapering off into pointed ornaments some way down. Then came a deep walled moat, once no doubt communicating with the river; but now cattle grazed comfortably there, and in and out of the grassy court. An inscription round the tower recorded the founder and his date; but rain had trickled over its handsome roseate letters—it seemed not too fanciful to trace there some resemblance to the bold calligraphy of the Arabs—and now all that could be read was some figures which might have been mcccclviii, or might not. There was no climbing the tower; but the guardian was not content till he had pulled us up on to the walls and led us along the brown slippery grass on the parapet—at no slight risk of a fall into the court below—to examine a *cubo* at close quarters. Down over the wall the little staircases led into these hanging turrets, with loopholes to command stretches of curtain-wall in two directions. It was a curious sensation to feel oneself outside the fortress and yet in the place of a defender and in shelter.

From the castle we turned into the town—if so shrunken a place could merit such a name. The *posada* did not invite to coffee, so we passed on up the small street, hung, as is usual in Spain even in the remotest villages, with electric light, just a single wire and a bulb of two or three candle power. In a small plot beside the church children were playing, despite the full blaze of the westering sun; and the brightest of them answered an enquiry for the keys by running off to fetch the sextoness. After a struggle with the lock she let us into a big barnlike structure, whitewashed beyond hope, and striking sharply cold after the heat outside. Here at length were the Tombs of the Fonsecas, four white marble effigies recumbent on long slabs which gave ample room for inscriptions—one in either transept, one north and one south of the altar. Eldest was Fernando de Fonseca (†1463), buried with his second wife, Mary of Ayala. The third, Alonso (†1505), was commemorated with his mother, Mary of Avellana. The youngest, Juan Rodriguez (†1524), son of Fernando, had been Archdeacon of Seville and head of the India House there, and had held a Calabrian archbishopric. At the India House he raised obstacles to thwart Columbus' third journey; but twenty years later as Bishop of Burgos he atoned for this to posterity by giving material aid to Magellan.

But it was the second who interested us most, Fernando's brother, an earlier Alonso who had been Archbishop of Seville (†May 18, 1473), and *primer fundador de esta casa.* Here was the reward of our trudge under the sun, the reward of our thirst. This Alonso had been the patron of Antonius Nebrissensis, that famous Spanish scholar who with Ximenes' support had placed Spain in the van of the contest for the Revival of Learning. Now the chronology of Antonius' life is unsettled, and depends on various statements which he makes incidentally in his works. He was born in 1444, the year before the civil strife at Olmedo, was so many years at Salamanca, went at nineteen to Bologna, then so many years with Fonseca, so many again at Salamanca, so many with Stunica (†1504), a later Archbishop of Seville; and when the figures are added together, they amount to too many, more than the sixty allowed by the limits given. For a midway point the date of Fonseca's death was wanted; and for this recognized authorities could give nothing more sure than 1473, with a query—not a date to reckon from, though a late manuscript in Madrid added May 18. But here on his tomb was an authority beyond which one need not seek, the date of his death graven securely on stone.

So though our Alonso of Toledo, the Primate, had been laid elsewhere, Coca had yielded one pearl of price— small indeed, but without reproach. On the back of an old hotel-bill we took notes of the four inscriptions and returned into the heat, which was now surprisingly grateful. The two miles to the station seemed short with the pearl in our possession; and after more red wine there was time to sit happily in the thickest pool of shade by the station and sleep. A slow train struggled in, and soon bore us on to Medina del Campo (where in another rose-red castle the great Catholic Queen Isabella died in 1504), welcome to us now for the flowing bowls of coffee and leisurely time to drink them. And so after sundown to royal Valladolid.

SIMANCAS

One smiles at thought of the richest treasure house of Spanish archives placed in a castle seven miles from a railway, carefully ordered and readily shown to those who can make their way to the plain village which offers no cheer to the visitor. But the high spirit of Spain has always been conservative. For nearly 400 years the archives have been there; why should they not remain?

Simancas stands above the ancient bridge which crosses the Pisuerga, and Ximenes built a castle there, to be a stronghold when the mutterings of the Comuneros storm were beginning to be clearly heard. The Admiral of Castile was to hold it, and thus strengthen the defences of royal Valladolid, which Ferdinand and Isabella loved so well, and to which Charles V brought his Empress for the birth of Philip II.

In 1542 it was resolved that this strong place should protect the archives of Castile, and a small chamber in the centre of the building, duly provided with wooden cupboards still existing, was set aside for their accommodation; much as the Sorbonne, when printing began, allotted a small room to house the new kind of book which the old-fashioned regarded with disdain.

The Admirals of Castile little thought that they had admitted within their walls an enemy invincible and relentless, who would slowly drive them out and leave them little more than foot-room throughout the building, except in the chapel, a windowless cave, also in the centre. The guardian leads one through fifty-four rooms, packed with bundles, and points out with pride the pigeon-hole with the accounts of that great fleet which would have subdued England to the faith, but for the accident of the west wind, the breath of autumn's being. From the top you look out over the plain where the Douro joins the Pisuerga; and then he takes you down to see the treasures exposed in the show-cases. The contract of marriage between Ferdinand and Isabella, and their wills; Don John's dispatch after Lepanto, with a chart of the ships as they went into action; maps and plans of important towns, one, boldly drawn, of Ocaña made for Isabella in 1503, another of Antwerp, with the descriptions in Flemish. Interesting to English people are letters of our princes—one from Arthur in November 1501, swearing to be good and true to the charming Catherine he has just married: the firm signature sets one thinking of the tomb in Worcester Cathedral, and the sad figure of the forlorn father at the head of it; a gloriously illuminated document of 1503 in which Henry VII contracts to marry Catherine to Arthur's brother; a letter of July 1509, after the coronation, which Henry VIII dutifully reports to his bride's parents. There are letters too from the artists who served the Spanish royal house, one from Pedro Pauolo Rubens, twenty-three from Titian; and finally there are richly painted chests for holding documents; fine bindings; important charters.

It is pleasant to drive out behind a pair of horses (if they weren't so thin!) in the cool of a mid-September morning. The archives are open from eight to two—not very convenient hours for the student who must come seven miles—but no doubt they were ordained in 1542. After a busy morning's work one emerges from the gateway at 2 to a bread and cheese lunch in any shade that can be found. We chose a spot beside the road, beneath an acacia; a fresh wind blowing away the dust of an occasional motor scampering by to Tordesillas or Salamanca. Across a small gully, bright with butterflies though its herbage was burnt brown, was a threshing-floor such as Ornan the Jebusite made. The threshing was done: ox, horse and mule, unmuzzled, had trodden out the corn; women had tossed it with spades to winnow chaff from grain. The heaps of corn high upon the earth had disappeared into sacks and been parted among their owners; and now only the great ridges of chaff remained, fifty yards long perhaps, and nine or ten feet high, one behind the other. A little way off on a sky-line framed by the acacia were two men lading chaff into carts; looking like the busy devils who poke the wicked about in the background of medieval Last Judgements. And at the end the patient oxen moved off under their mountainous loads.

As we gazed, a faint shimmer of purple caught the eye. 'Something in the soil' we said, for there are streaks of mineral about; but when we came closer, it was a field of tiny crocuses, showing their heads and nothing more.

Through the trodden ground of the threshing-floor, a hard flat crust, still strewn with leavings of grain and chaff, these tender petals had come to redeem the hopeless aridity of the outlook: one of the compensations which nature loves to make, when she seems at her most cruel. Hundreds and thousands there were, bright and fresh, though not a trace of green was near them—only dust and brown earth and burnt wisps of grass. It was in truth a landscape which merited the misused word 'weird'. Above the stubble-plains of the near slopes rose rounded hills, scored with rain-tracks of winter, but offering no sign of life except a single hardy tree here and there. Yet it was not only the absence of life: the colour of these strange hills, to which it seemed the foot of man could never climb, suggested nothing else but death, death long ago. Wan they were, like the faces of dead men, or like mountains in the moon. As the eye roamed across the landscape, there was the green of the pine groves beside the Pisuerga; above these came the brown of the fields, already being ploughed up for next year, and higher, scarcely of the earth, were these pale ghosts of mountains wrapped as it were in grave-clothes.

We turned into the village leaving this queerly attractive scene of line and colour. The hills had been so when Ximenes built his castle, and when the church was raised —with its fine old tower like those of Santa Maria Antigua or San Martin in Valladolid, and the graceful lines of its choir and buttresses—to serve the spiritual needs of the guardians of the bridge. The life we saw seemed almost as old as the neighbour hills, like the life of the immemorial East. The walls of sun-dried brick, the narrow winding streets coming suddenly to an end and no way through, the mingling of men and animals, the reliance on the sun to purge man's uncleanliness—all recalled the life of an Indian village. The Plaza was full of dust, so that one could scarcely see across it: the reason soon appeared—masons were mending a roof, and casting the debris they made into the street by basketsful, without any form of warning.

From such a comfortless scene, the home of the lonely, almost exiled, archivists, it was a pleasure to turn the horses homewards to a city with a water-supply and other conveniences. But as we made haste to escape from dust and heat and smell, there came the thought of Froude working for months in this rich treasure house, regardless of what so oppressed us, if thereby he might make his History more real and living by drawing the inspiration of actual letters and dispatches which no English historian had ever seen; handling, copying, extracting, and catching that sense of almost personal intercourse which issues from autograph letters. And for this faithfulness, what was his reward?

PROVINS

A MEDIEVAL SANCTUARY

In the Middle Ages the Counts of Champagne made alternate visits to their two capitals, Troyes and Provins; following the food supply, administering justice, regulating the fairs, and organizing the strength and protection which were the essence of the feudal tie, and made the service which it required of lesser men thankfully rendered. But Troyes was always the first. It had its bishop and its cathedral, with lofty columns soaring to the roof in unbroken line, and enriched in the thirteenth century with wonderful stained glass which has survived the various destroyers of later days. There, too, a shoemaker's son, turned Pope, built on the site of his father's shop a church which seems to have more glass in its walls

than stone—at a time when English builders were only
learning to put five plain lancets together to form an
east window. In Troyes, after the Treaty, our Henry V
married Katherine of France; and when the sixteenth
century came, what an outbreak there was of church
building or decoration—the massive west front of the
cathedral and its one great tower, the *jubé* of the Made-
leine, the Calvary of St. Nicholas and its imposing stair-
case. The library of Troyes, too, has remarkable riches.
At the Revolution the books of thirty-six religious houses
were swept into it, including those of Clairvaux, with
St. Bernard's Bible and notes from his own hand in the
margins.

Yet, to lovers of the past, Provins, the second of the
two, shall be first. To it have come no modern prosperity
to transform into ugliness, no circus housed under a large
dome, no factories, no clanging tram-bells, not even a
large railway-station, only one of those country halting-
places which seem made for rest and friendliness rather
than for anxious bustle and noise. Troyes has increased,
Provins has decreased. The space within its ramparts
is no longer filled with houses; fields and gardens run up
to the inner side of its walls, and only the mouths of
cellars here and there, or striking well-heads, their stones
worn by the ropes, record that once men dwelt above.
But what remains is almost all of the Middle Age. Here
is a house in which St. Thibaut, son of Count Arnould,
was born in 1017; there the Hôtel Dieu, founded by
Count Henry the Liberal, in 1160; and the tithe-barn
which he gave to the Chapter, with vaulted roof and
vaulted cellars below, all of the twelfth century or earlier,
except for a gallery of almost continuous window, broken
through in the days of Nicholas Durand of Villegagnon,
'first seaman of his age', born in the town when our

Henry VIII was a 'divine' young King. The barn is now a museum; and among its treasures are Merovingian sarcophagi with herringbone ornament, brought in from the country near—one inscribed in curious minuscule with the name of Genesius presbyter, the other holding the sword of a warrior—which were old when St. Thibaut ran about the narrow streets as a child. From its basement steps bring one to a network of *souterrains*, connecting with all parts of the upper town; roughly hewn through the rock, and too low for ordinary heads, though the nimble little guide darts like an arrow through one dark opening after another. Elsewhere are the Hôtel de Vauluisant, its vaulted cellars now stabling horses, and the thirteenth-century small cause Court. On the summit of the ridge stands the Church of St. Quiriace, once as great as a cathedral, great even now when most of its nave has gone and its crossing is crowned with an ugly dome. Beside it the *donjon*, a solid mass of twelfth-century masonry, flanked with four later tourelles—the castle of the masters and the prison of not a few French nobles who came in the masters' way.

Around all this lie the ramparts, long stretches of them as perfect as when they kept the English out; though wallflowers now grow where the archers stood, and the moat is planted with fruit trees, and violets hide at their feet. Tower follows tower with the most modern inventions of their day, full fifty feet from summit to fosse; and there are sallyports and long stairways leading down to them through the rock. One dark October night in 1432 the English cannon made a breach even in these formidable lines, the enemy poured in, and for a time Provins was no longer French. Holding the town, they made the *donjon* doubly strong, building a huge round wall, in which the old tower seems to sit as in a great

pie-dish—'paté des Anglais', it is still called, and the
ramparts still show 'the English breach'.

But those days are over. 'Les Anglais are now our
friends,' said the stout *gardien*. 'When the Boche came
that September morning—only six kilometres away, and
he said he would take his déjeuner at the Boule d'Or, on
his way to Paris—les Anglais attacked him at Coulom-
miers and we', pointing with his arm, 'attacked him
there, and he was swept away, back from the Marne to
the Aisne. Yes, Monsieur, les Anglais are now our
friends.'

MONTBENOÎT

As you step out of the station at Montbenoît you
wonder what you have come out for to see. A broad
valley of open, smiling fields, pine-topped towards
Switzerland, pine-topped towards France, but scarcely
a building in view; only the little Doubs, dry almost to
extinction in this parched summer, wandering in a cleft
below, as he sets out on his tortuous career, to make a
citadel for Besançon, and then lose himself in the Saône
and the Rhone and the sea. But go a few yards towards
him, and a spire appears above the edge of the bed he
has cut through these level Jura strata: showing where
a village nestles into the steep bank. A few steps more,
and it is all at your feet; first the church, beyond, the
inn and the post-office, and around them half a cluster
of houses. The church greets you with its choir, like
St. Pierre at Tonnerre, familiar to all who go south by
the P.L.M., superb upon its rock surveying the town
below. But at Tonnerre it is a slender, fourteenth-
century choir, with tall windows, while the rest has been
transformed into the spacious Renaissance architecture
so much fancied in Burgundy and Champagne in the

later sixteenth century. At Montbenoît every line of the choir tells subtly of the Renaissance coming: the tracery is a shade more flamboyant than the fifteenth century would have allowed, the buttresses are slightly curved and fluted, and over all is a richly-pierced parapet, curiously placed under the roof. Farther west the church is plain twelfth century, as it was first built; and many feet below, because Doubs' bank is steep, clings to it a tiny cloister, scarcely larger than that of Cavaillon in Provence, with its columns so small that a single stone will serve as capital for two—the most notable of the capitals being a long fish.

In this quiet valley, such as the contemplative orders loved, a member of the family of Joux near Pontarlier, built a new Augustinian house about 1150, for the peace of his soul and his parents'. It had no distinguished record; but after three and a half centuries it fell into the hands of the son of a Chancellor of Burgundy. This new commendatory abbot, Ferry Carondelet, was a gay, attractive spirit, who when his young wife died before he was twenty-five, sought solace in the career ecclesiastic. Returning to his law studies at Bologna he proceeded doctor; fitting himself to represent Burgundian interests at the court of Julius II. Meanwhile he gathered up an archdeaconry at Besançon, a provostship at Furnes, rich benefices and 'pensions' in many directions. In Italy he had himself painted by Raphael, in that striking portrait which the Duke of Grafton allowed London to see a few years ago; and an even more engaging presentment of him is in 'La Vierge des Carondelets', painted by Fra Bartolommeo di Viterbo, and now hanging in the cathedral of Besançon. Below the Virgin and Child, Ferry kneels there, with his name-saint, St. Ferjeux, the apostle of Besançon, behind him, and St. Sebastian opposite.

What gives the picture a piquant interest is a scene thrust into its midst—not a view through a window, such as Italians love, of green hills far away—but a sudden opening, between the Virgin above and her kneeling worshipper, where structurally no window ever was. Through it may be seen a group of youths, naked as for bathing and with their backs turned, some standing, some sitting by the side of a river ; at one side is a balustraded bridge, beyond are woods, with one tree rising above the rest into a deep blue sky. What is intended no one can tell: M. Castan, who has made a careful study of the picture, conjectures that Ferry may have wished to commemorate, as with an *ex-voto*, some providential deliverance from drowning in an Italian river.

Montbenoît was given to him when he was nearly forty. Some ten years later, about 1520, he conceived the project of rebuilding its dark old church, with ideas from the beautiful Italy in which most of his life had been spent. Just at the same time, seventy miles away to the south-west, sad Margaret of Austria was raising her wonderful church at Brou to enshrine her grief, with Flemish workmen skilled in their arts of masonry, and wood-carvers from Savoy. Ferry's architect was perhaps a Frenchman, son of the printer Badius ; but his workmen within must have been Italian, so delicate is their ornament on the stalls and the stone canopies and arches. Airy, graceful, light, the flowers and tendrils twine about, in marked contrast to the rotund lines of later Renaissance work, bulging with lozenges and cherubs and fat twisted columns. The woodwork has an almost Muhammadan austerity in the absence of human figures: though the few scenes presented, Samson and Delilah, Campaspe and Aristotle, and a woman dragging her rival backwards by the hair, are remarkable. Ferry himself appears quite artlessly at every turn. In August 1522 Parneta Mesnier, a little girl of fourteen who was helping in the work, fell off the scaffolding and was killed: a tablet in the nave records her virtue and that Ferry wished her name remembered. East of the stalls, on the north wall, is a monument to the first founders, the de Joux, a knight with visor raised, upon a placid horse; the first words of the inscription announce that Ferry put it up in 1525. Against the south wall is a wide archway set, very beautiful, to encompass the Abbot's throne of 1526. Here again his name stands first; and later we are told that the seat was placed for the glory of God and the convenience of the Abbot's successors. The last date that can now be read in Ferry's work is 1527—the church has just been made a *Monument historique*, and until happier times return, much has been boarded up, discretion being the better part of architecture. Within a year Ferry was dead, and a successor came to try the convenience of his seat. We may forgive the slight vanity which led him into such prominence, for the historical sense which has made it possible to date with precision so charming a piece of early Renaissance church decoration.

THANN

The first thing you see in Thann is the Rue 7 Août. On that great day in 1914 French troops entered the town, and thereafter, much enduring for four years and more, it has remained French. Down the valley you come even now to 'pill-boxes' and heaps of barbed wire; but they face west, resisting advance into the plain from the Ballon d'Alsace and the Hartmannsweilerkopf, which are not far off, with Thann in the line of fire. 'You see, Monsieur, this was the principal theatre of the War.'

This may or may not be true—one has heard the words
uttered elsewhere—but Thann has other claims to attention. Its position on the road from Paris to Basle gave
it importance far back in the Middle Ages. The castle is
gone, the round tower, toppled over by Turenne in 1674,
lying like part of an enormous cask. But despite the
cross-firing of the War, the church, St. Thibaut's of
Provins, rebuilt in the fifteenth century after destruc-
tions of the town by the English in 1376 and by the
Armagnacs in 1445, still stands intact. Even Meiseer
Remigius Walch's fine spire, completed in 1511, has
escaped, though houses fell on its right hand and on
its left. The tall, slender choir shelters beneath the
tower: with two finely vaulted aisles the minster,
profusely decorated within and without, is scarcely
more than a parish church. In 1915 the French prudently removed its great treasures, the glass and the
carved stalls; and thus they are unhurt and back in
their places to-day, when much beside them has gone
to the ground.

The fifteenth-century glass is rich in colour, with
designs large enough to be clearly seen. Most remarkable
is one on the north, showing the days of the Creation:
first a kaleidoscopic view of queerly shaped masses falling together to make an earth; then an armful of great
lights, and stars bursting from a cloud, not a little en-
cumbering their Maker; then a golden land being marked
off from a silver sea most precisely with a compass; the
flowers and the animals after their kinds; and finally
Adam, alive from the waist up, having a right arm
fitted on.

But where else can such wood-carving be seen? Many
greater churches rejoice in their stalls and show
wonderful designs in time-blackened oak; also much

figure-work which is only mediocre. But the artist who
came to Thann—his name is unknown: for men lived in
pockets then, as men do still, the faculties mixing but
rarely, so that none of the polygraphic humanists took
heed of his modern skill—this artist put life into the wood,
till one can almost think that the figures move. In every
line his fancy speaks, not an opportunity wasted. At any
turn in the elaborate canopies an unexpected face may
appear, and yet the symmetry is not lost. But when the
chisel is turned to things animate, a sudden reality comes.
There is a note of harshness, almost of savagery, in some
of the monsters, with their rough skins and gruesome
faces. But with humans the master is usually gentle;
and in a few rapid strokes there is life almost breathing.
A young mother bowing tenderly over her child. A figure
blown along in the wind, its robes flying; clutching with
one bare foot, muscles standing out in the effort, at a big
stone as it passes. A man climbing, the left hand—
stretched back over his head—grasping a rock almost
out of reach, the left foot standing tiptoe; while the
right knee, lifted as far as it will go, presses with the right
hand against the cliff, striving for support by mere force
of adhesion—every muscle tense, till you can almost hear
him pant in his fearful struggle.

Down below, from the upper rows of stalls to the lower,
the bench-ends descend in flowing curves which make
a sort of bank. Each has its figure—some ten master-
pieces, showing how men sit on such sloping ground—
a pedlar, pack on back, stretching out his weary legs to
their full; a boy, leaning slightly to one side, with one
knee drawn up, the other straight down, his hands idly
before him; a young man, straining in thought, legs
crossed below the knee, arms behind him straight to the
ground, bearing his weight alert; an old man in gentle

reverie, his toes turned inwards across one another; a monk reading intently from a book, a nun from a long scroll; a fat bald-headed Mr. Pickwick, in abbot's dress, and a pair of large round spectacles.

In the stalls themselves figures stand everywhere, in generous profusion, down the uprights, and in unexpected corners. A pair of apes sit back to back, looking up with the whimsical air of those trying a new attitude; a Gruffanuff with head squeezed down to his legs; on the provost's chair two queer contorted figures with human faces; even at the end of the unseen shelf to carry books, where surely a carver might have thought his work was done, the face and watchful eyes of a large dog.

We do not know his name, this master who could do what he liked with the wood; but then no more do we of a hundredth part of those into whose labours we have entered. To our unknown benefactors!

HUNGARY REVISITED

For those who have been in India it is not easy in this climate of ours to recall our past experience. Warren Hastings in his greenhouses at Daylesford could simulate the atmosphere of Bengal. Sometimes too after drought a sudden shower raises here that delicate scent of an earth grateful and refreshed which marks the beginning of the monsoon. But for the most part England is too green. Even in July 1921, when the sun had the victory, it was not India that met our gaze, harvested lands drinking in the heat to cherish next year's seeds, but green fields burnt brown and even silvery white, as though leprous, to be passed with averted eyes. Nature's trials for us are frost and storm and snow, the ceaseless rain or the wayward variety which needs the faithful witness in heaven; not the pitiless skies of burning brass, nor those

D d

dread nights when the low dust-clouds hang over one like the lid of a saucepan.

But go to the plains of Hungary and you may see again 'the infinite recession of a Punjab horizon'. July there is like the cold weather of Northern India; not the winter of Lahore, where a man may spread at nightfall a thousand bowls of water, and at sunrise gather crescent globes of ice, to be stored below ground till summer comes again, but the cold weather of Allahabad or Benares, which know not the extremes of higher latitudes. Hungary will give the same assured blue sky without a cloud; the far-off hills sleeping in the morning sun, and fading away as the air grows thick in the heat; the silence of noon when man rests beneath the trees and no birds sing; the floods of golden light as the sun knoweth his going down; the young moon hanging serene in the sky, its old parent in its arms, while the stars come softly out and the white buildings throw off their unexpected light; and dawn with its delicious cool that needs a blanket.

Around one is much that seems familiar. The swart southern peasants marching sturdily along the *cutcha* roads, barefooted but their heads carefully wrapped up; the golden crops so early garnered; the maize standing high in the fields; the bridges where no water runs in the courses; the gate-posts standing without fence or wall, and no gates hanging between; oxen and even buffaloes toiling in their wagons under huge loads of straw; sheep first seen in the distance along the road as a low cloud of thin dust; lizards darting in beneath the stones, or up the loose-built walls of sun-dried brick; hoopoes whirring by, and orioles calling from the flowering trees; and for those that like them there are dust-storms and mosquitoes. To visit a village notable you step through a wall almost as high as a purdah garden, over a door-sill of eight inches or a foot, and find before you not a garden of lawns and beds, but a dusty enclosure, shaded by one big tree and garnished in its corners by little stands of pot-plants, such as the Indian *mali* and *bhishti* cherish with all their minds.

Hungary is no happy land to-day. The race that with the Poles spilt its blood for centuries in protecting the eastern frontiers of Europe against Mongol and Tartar and Turk is now divided in spite of itself; and the renascent nations around them seem more likely to repeat the mistakes of 1871 than to win cohesion by magnanimity. Leyden University has a charitable foundation, dating back to the seventeenth century, to help Protestant students from Hungary and Transylvania; and this may now have a new usefulness. But the Hungarians are not apt to give way. In the face of many vexations, small and great, they are standing their ground with dignity, confident that the public opinion of Europe, when once informed, will not tolerate the persecution of one of its proudest nations.

DURHAM

For nine hundred years Durham has been an outpost of England. After the collapse of Roman government and the breaching of the Wall, the north lay open again to invaders, coming to raid and to destroy. Picts and Scots, Norsemen from over the sea, vexed the land and there was none to help. In 875 Danes drove Cuthbert's monks from Lindisfarne, and for seven years they wandered with their Saint's body in its wooden coffin, quaintly incised with letters runic and roman. After a century's shelter in the old Roman stronghold at Chester-le-Street another invasion sent them wandering again

with their precious burden; until in 997 the Saint in his
coffin, or some monk with an eye for a good position,
bade them halt on the defensible rock almost insulated
by a big bend of the Wear. And there their monastery
was refounded, to endure until a later age found the
institution out of date. So strong was the rock that
seventy years later the Conqueror on visiting it exclaimed at once, 'Let there be a Castle'; and so a castle
was added, with perhaps the oldest bit of Norman building in this country, and over both monastery and
castle the Bishop held sway. By good fortune one of
Rufus' bishops, Carileph, had to fly from that irascible
king; and, while in exile, beheld the great churches which
were rising in Normandy, at Caen and Rouen and where
not. Having made his peace, he set to work to emulate
what he had seen; Flambard followed, and the monks
seconding him well, the church of Durham was soon
complete, except for the adornments of a century or
more later, culminating in the splendid central tower,
rebuilt by Prior William of Ebchester during the Wars
of the Roses.

But though castle and monastery were secure upon
their rock, it was a troubled land around; suitable enough
for Guderic—the *pirata de regno Angliae* who with his
ship had helped King Baldwin out of a tight place in
Palestine in 1102—to found his hermitage at Finchale,
when home from the sea; but not the place for men with
wives and children who wished to live peaceably in their
habitations and labour with their hands upon Mother
Earth. So the Bishop was created a Palatine, and was
entrusted by the King with keeping the frontier, with
the help of the New Castle on the Tyne, and Norham,
and other fortresses along the line; while nobles made
them castles of their own, Bamburgh and Lumley and

Brancepeth and many another. Yet with all this there was no peace. The Scots came and went, and the English did the same over the Border. On 17 October 1346 King David was met by Bishop Hatfield with the Archbishop of York and the Nevilles; who vanquished him on a hill across the Wear, while the Prior, like Moses at Rephidim, held up the Standard of St. Cuthbert on another hill near by. The Scottish banners were set up in the Cathedral for tokens; and a cross was built, to bear the name of the Nevilles, even after reforming zeal has robbed it of its emblem. To another bishop, Ruthall, came the glory of Flodden Field, the 'reward of the piety' of Henry VIII, who was just then occupied in grabbing Tournay. With Bishop Tunstall the power of the Palatine began to wane, as the Border became less disturbed; but traces of that high jurisdiction—the Bishop's Judge and the power of life and death—lasted down to the nineteenth century, almost within living memory. For the aged Canon is only just dead who could remember seeing Bishop Van Mildert's staff of office as Count Palatine broken and thrown into his grave in 1836.

In another manner Durham was an outpost for England. The finest tradition of English learning had been brought in when Carileph ejected the seculars of Lindisfarne and established the Benedictines of Jarrow and Wearmouth, fortified with the bones of Bede, in case the seculars should claim to carry off with them the virtues and the miracles of Cuthbert; and this credit was maintained by Prior John of Darlington (†1284), who made the first English Concordance to the Bible, and by Bishop Richard of Bury, author of *Philobiblon*. The monastery devoted much of its energies to the writing and the study of manuscripts, and the bishops presented many. One of Carileph's has a portrait of himself. Hugh of Pudsey's

Bible, almost as beautiful in its way as his Galilee, was so gloriously illuminated that the cupidity of lesser men cut out many of the initial letters for scrapbooks. The monks' standards of what was fitting rose so high that even their manuscripts of canon law—procured for use and not for ornament—had gorgeous initials to each little section. What the monks read may be gathered from the Catalogue made by careful Brother William of Appleby in 1391, when he succeeded to the charge of the Library in place of a Brother who had been transferred to the Feretory. The books were in three places; some in the Spendement or Chancery whence the monastery payments were made, others in the cloister, others again in the refectory. It was a rich library, with numbers of Bibles, complete or in parts—Psalters and Prophets and Gospels; Fathers of the Church and Schoolmen; Lives of the Saints, Guderic of course among them; and not a few of the Latin classics. Brother William gives lists also of books sent to Oxford in 1406, for the use of Durham College, now Trinity; and of others that went to Stamford in 1422.

When printing came the new art was valued in Durham. Bishop Shirwood, who had been employed by the King in Rome, bought there as they came out, many of the splendid volumes of Sweynheym and Pannartz, and others of Jenson and Wendelin of Spires from Venice; half a dozen Ciceros, Plutarch's Lives in Latin, which he read right through, Livy and Suetonius and Josephus, Horace and Statius and Martial, Vitruvius and Frontinus on the Aqueducts, Jerome and Lactantius. At just the same time the Prior, John of Auckland, also made a collection of books, which in time found their way to the library, all in manuscript and almost all medieval. Why Shirwood's books did not go to the monks is not clear: possibly a Prior of so different a temperament would not accept them. Their fortune was to pass to his successor, Bishop Fox, who gave them later to his new trilingual college of Corpus Christi in Oxford.

Of Tunstall's books a few are still in Durham; but most of them have wandered elsewhere. That generous person, a leader in toleration, gave some away in his lifetime. Others—best of them all, a copy, specially printed for him on vellum, of Erasmus' New Testament— are at York; in the collections of Archbishop Toby Matthew, sometime Dean of Durham, which were presented to the Minster by that admirable woman his wife; daughter, daughter-in-law, wife, and sister-in-law to seven bishops and archbishops.

Tunstall's spirit was reflected in his chaplain and secretary, Robert Ridley, whom he brought with him from St. Paul's. In 1533-4, only a few years before the Dissolution, Ridley enriched the monks—whom he must surely have deemed likely and ready to profit by it— with a handsome gift of many of the new editions of the Fathers; the Froben Jerome of 1516 and Ambrose of 1527, the former bound by the Cambridge bookbinder Garret Godfrey; the Chevallon Augustine of 1523, and a Complutensian Polyglott, four volumes of which have unaccountably wandered off to Hereford. Another notable addition, gift of one of the first new Prebendaries after the monks had gone, is the Froben Augustine of 1529 in ten volumes, all labelled on their sides and elaborately bossed for lying on desks instead of standing on shelves—as late an example as may be found of the spacious medieval method of library arrangement.

In 1657 Cromwell was for erecting the castle into a college; but as with another and greater project of to-day, hostility to the man thwarted his good scheme, and the older universities fostered the ungenerous opposition. Bishop Cosin collected a great library; and then in 1832—out of due time, for its growth was to be retarded by the invention of railways—Durham became the University of Northern England. Van Mildert gave it the castle with all its architectural treasures as a habitation; in 1855 Routh, the almost centenarian President of Magdalen, bequeathed another fine library as some atonement for what Oxford had done two centuries before; and such benefactions continue. At Newcastle another college is doing active work; and so the university lives and thrives, England's outpost in the north.

Those that vainly talk against the League of Nations, averring that 'you cannot change human nature', would do well to visit these lands upon the Border. No more the Scot with his bag of oatmeal and his untiring pony raids and lifts and escapes free; no more do English Lieutenants exult at having 'destroyed six good towns'; no more will Durham's Cathedral serve as prison for 3,500 Scots marched all the way down from Dunbar. No faster friends now than Scots and English at peace.

INDEX

E e

PRINTED IN GREAT BRITAIN AT THE UNIVERSITY PRESS, OXFORD
BY JOHN JOHNSON, PRINTER TO THE UNIVERSITY